ppy Birthday   Merry Christmas   For You On Mother's Day   Get Well Soon   Congratulations
shing You A Very Happy Easter   Sorry I Forgot Your Birthday
reting   Be My Valentine   Hope Your Halloween Is Haunted   He   day
niversary Celebration   Just Because I Love You   Rejoicing The Birth Of Your Baby   Happy Birthday
rry Christmas   For You On Mother's Day   Get Well Soon   Congratulations   Wishing You A Very
appy Easter   Sorry I Forgot Your Birthday   Bon Voyage   A Belated Birthday Greeting   Be My
lentine   Hope Your Halloween Is Haunted   Here's To You Dad   For Your Anniversary Celebration
st Because I Love You   Rejoicing The Birth Of Your Baby   Happy Birthday   Merry Christmas   For
u On Mother's Day   Get Well Soon   Congratulations   Wishing You A Very Happy Easter   Sorry I
orgot Your Birthday   Bon Voyage   A Belated Birthday Greeting   Be My Valentine   Hope Your
alloween Is Haunted   Here's To You Dad   For Your Anniversary Celebration   Just Because I Love
u   Rejoicing The Birth Of Your Baby   Happy Birthday   Merry Christmas   For You On Mother's
ay   Get Well Soon   Congratulations   Wishing You A Very Happy Easter   Sorry I Forgot Your
rthday   Bon Voyage   A Belated Birthday Greeting   Be My Valentine   Hope Your Halloween Is
aunted   Here's To You Dad   For Your Anniversary Celebration   Just Because I Love You   Rejoicing
he Birth Of Your Baby   Happy Birthday   Merry Christmas   For You On Mother's Day   Get Well
oon   Congratulations   Wishing You A Very Happy Easter   Sorry I Forgot Your Birthday   Bon
oyage   A Belated Birthday Greeting   Be My Valentine   Hope Your Halloween Is Haunted   Here's To
u Dad   For Your Anniversary Celebration   Just Because I Love You   Rejoicing The Birth Of Your
aby   Happy Birthday   Merry Christmas   For You On Mother's Day   Get Well Soon
ongratulations   Wishing You A Very Happy Easter   Sorry I Forgot Your Birthday   Bon Voyage   A
elated Birthday Greeting   Be My Valentine   Hope Your Halloween Is Haunted   Here's To You Dad
or Your Anniversary Celebration   Just Because I Love You   Rejoicing The Birth Of Your Baby
appy Birthday   Merry Christmas   For You On Mother's Day   Get Well Soon   Congratulations
ishing You A Very Happy Easter   Sorry I Forgot Your Birthday   Bon Voyage   A Belated Birthday
reeting   Be My Valentine   Hope Your Halloween Is Haunted   Here's To You Dad   For Your
nniversary Celebration   Just Because I Love You   Rejoicing The Birth Of Your Baby   Happy Birthday
rry Christmas   For You On Mother's Day   Get Well Soon   Congratulations   Wishing You A Very
appy Easter   Sorry I Forgot Your Birthday   Bon Voyage   A Belated Birthday Greeting   Be My
alentine   Hope Your Halloween Is Haunted   Here's To You Dad   For Your Anniversary Celebration
st Because I Love You   Rejoicing The Birth Of Your Baby   Happy Birthday   Merry Christmas   For
ou On Mother's Day   Get Well Soon   Congratulations   Wishing You A Very Happy Easter   Sorry I
orgot Your Birthday   Bon Voyage   A Belated Birthday Greeting   Be My Valentine   Hope Your
alloween Is Haunted   Here's To You Dad   For Your Anniversary Celebration   Just Because I Love
ou   Rejoicing The Birth Of Your Baby   Happy Birthday   Merry Christmas   For You On Mother's
ay   Get Well Soon   Congratulations   Wishing You A Very Happy Easter   Sorry I Forgot Your
irthday   Bon Voyage   A Belated Birthday Greeting   Be My Valentine   Hope Your Halloween Is
aunted   Here's To You Dad   For Your Anniversary Celebration   Just Because I Love You   Rejoicin
he Birth Of Your Baby   Happy Birthday   Merry Christmas   For You On Mother's Day   Get Well
oon   Congratulations   Wishing You A Very Happy Easter   Sorry I Forgot Your Birthday   Bon
oyage   A Belated Birthday Greeting   Be My Valentine   Hope Your Halloween Is Haunted   Here's To
u Dad   For Your Anniversary Celebration   Just Because I Love You   Rejoicing The Birth Of Your
aby   Happy Birthday   Merry Christmas   For You On Mother's Day   Get Well Soon
ongratulations   Wishing You A Very Happy Easter   Sorry I Forgot Your Birthday   Bon Voyage   A
elated Birthday Greeting   Be My Valentine   Hope Your Halloween Is Haunted   Here's To You Dad
or Your Anniversary Celebration   Just Because I Love You   Rejoicing The Birth Of Your Baby
appy Birthday   Merry Christmas   For You On Mother's Day   Get Well Soon   Congratulations
ishing You A Very Happy Easter   Sorry I Forgot Your Birthday   Bon Voyage   A Belated Birthday

CREATIVE CRAFTING WITH RECYCLED GREETING CARDS

Catherine Lawrence

Sterling Publishing Co., Inc. New York
A Sterling Chapelle Book

For Chapelle, Ltd.

Owner: Jo Packham

Editor: Malissa Moody Boatwright

Staff: Marie Barber, Kass Burchett, Rebecca Christensen, Holly Fuller, Marilyn Goff, Michael Hannah, Shirley Heslop, Holly Hollingsworth, Susan Jorgensen, Pauline Locke, Ginger Mikkelsen, Barbara Milburn, Linda Orton, Karmen Quinney, Leslie Ridenour, and Cindy Stoeckl

Photographer: Kevin Dilley for Hazen Photography

Photography Styling: Susan Laws

Designers: Sharon Ganske, Kelly Henderson, Chizuko Heslop, Jo Packham, Jamie Pierce, Rhonda Rainey, and Cindy Rooks

If you have any questions or comments or would like information on specialty products featured in this book, please contact: Chapelle, Ltd. • P.O. Box 9252 • Ogden, UT 84409 (801) 621-2777 • Fax (801) 621-2788

Due to the limited amount of space available, we must print our patterns at a reduced size in order to give our patrons the maximum number of patterns possible in our publications. We believe the quality and quantity of our patterns will compensate for any inconvenience this may cause.

The written instructions, photographs, designs, patterns, and projects in this volume are intended for the personal use of the reader and may be reproduced for that purpose only. Any other use, especially commercial use, is forbidden under law without the written permission of the copyright holder.

Every effort has been made to ensure that all the information in this book is accurate. However, due to differing conditions, tools, and individual skills, the publisher cannot be responsible for any injuries, losses, and other damages which may result from the use of the information in this book.

Library of Congress Cataloging-in-Publication Data

Lawrence, Catherine
    Creative crafting with recycled greeting cards / Catherine Lawrence.
        p.   cm.
    "A Sterling/Chapelle book."
    Includes index.
    ISBN 0-8069-9825-3
    1. Handicraft.   2. Greeting cards.   3. Recycling (Waste, etc.)
I. Title
TT157.L325   1997
745.5--dc21   97-22141
                                                 CIP

10 9 8 7 6 5 4 3 2 1

First paperback edition published in 1998 by
Sterling Publishing Company, Inc.
387 Park Avenue South, New York, N.Y. 10016
© 1997 by Chapelle, Ltd.
Distributed in Canada by Sterling Publishing
% Canadian Manda Group, One Atlantic Avenue, Suite 105
Toronto, Ontario, Canada M6K 3E7
Distributed in Great Britain and Europe by Cassell PLC
Wellington House, 125 Strand, London WC2R 0BB, England
Distributed in Australia by Capricorn Link (Australia) Pty Ltd.
P.O. Box 6651, Baulkham Hills, Business Centre, NSW 2153, Australia
Printed in Hong Kong
All rights reserved

Sterling ISBN 0-8069-9825-3 Trade
              0-8069-9826-1 Paper

Projects shown in this publication were created with the outstanding and innovative products developed by the following companies:

Aleene's Paints, Crafter's Goop, Loctite Glue, Offray Ribbon, Plaid Paints, *and* **Sakura Hobby Craft.**

We would like to offer our sincere appreciation to these companies for the valuable support given in this ever changing industry of new ideas, concepts, designs, and products.

All the names
I know from
nurse:
Gardener's
garters,
Shepherd's
purse,
Bachelor's
buttons,

Lady's smock, And the
Lady Hollyhock.
Fairy places, fairy things,
Fairy woods where the wild bee
wings,

Tiny trees for
tiny dames –
These must all
be fairy names!

Robert Louis Stevenson

Cards On Canvas
Instructions on page 94

47

56

41

60

81

25

Celestial Insights

32

23

61

100

Contents

66

49

104

General Instructions

Before Beginning

Before beginning, select the theme of the card. Once the theme of a card has been decided upon, coordinate all materials (acrylic paint, charms, embellishments, fabric, markers, papers, and pens) needed to complete the project.

Use the projects in this book as inspiration for the many different ways greeting cards can be transformed into delightful crafts and home decorations. The possibilities are endless. Have fun and be creative!!

Before using any of the tools and/or materials listed in this book, or for specific questions, be certain to read and follow manufacturer's instructions.

Alternative cards are shown below each project title that could be used in place of the card used on the model projects in this book. Alternative cards are also shown at the end of specific project instructions to give additional ideas. These cards and ideas are labeled "In Other Words."

Acrylic Spray Sealer

Most of the projects in this book were sealed with an acrylic spray sealer. However, there are optional brush-on sealers available. The crafter should use the type they prefer.

The different types of acrylic spray sealers are either matte sealer, for flat finish; satin sealer, for semi-gloss finish; or clear sealer, for gloss finish. Any type can be used depending on the look that is desired.

Baking Clay

Baking clay (polymer sculpting, modeling compound) has excellent handling qualities. It is soft and pliable, and can be baked in a home oven. It takes tooling (drilling, sanding, and painting) well and can be rolled and cut.

Baking clay is available in a variety of colors, or white clay may be used then painted.

Knead clay until soft and smooth. Mold and sculpt clay into required form.

Use paintbrush end, toothpick or wire, and knife to assist in making indentations, score lines, paint lines and, if needed, to help support clay during sculpting.

Remove clay form from project. Place clay form on aluminum foil and bake clay.

After object has cooled, apply acrylic gesso to object before acrylic paint is applied.

Cutting Tools

Designate a special pair of scissors for cutting paper and fabric. Using your fabric scissors to cut other materials will dull the blades and make them less effective for fabric cutting.

•Craft Knife

Good for cutting foam board, felt, paper, vinyl, and many other craft materials. Make certain blade is sharp.

•Paper Edger Scissors

Create decorative corners and edges for cards. Each pair of paper edgers cuts a different design.

•Craft Scissors

Use 4" craft scissors for very detailed cutting of paper, cloth, thread, tape, string, and many other craft materials.

Use 4" curved craft scissors for cutting cloth, yarn, ribbon, and many other craft materials flush against a surface.

Use 5" craft scissors for precision cutting of cloth, tape, string, paper, and many other craft materials.

Use 8" craft scissors for cutting cloth, tape, string, paper, and many other craft materials.

Use 8" multi-layer scissors for cutting multiple layers of fabric, felt, and many other craft materials.

Fabric-Covering Tips

Place fabric on working surface wrong side up.

Apply craft glue to fabric. Place and smooth fabric to frame. Be certain fabric is entirely adhered to all edges of frame.

Trim off excess fabric if needed.

Glue
•Adhesive & Sealant

Adhesive & sealant is stronger than craft glue. It dries clear, is waterproof, flexible, and paintable.

Apply to both surfaces, wait five minutes, and press both surfaces together. Adhesive & sealant sets in about 10 minutes.

Use only in well-ventilated area.

•Clear Silicone

Clear silicone can be used to raise cut out artwork away from background for a 3-dimensional appearance.

Squeeze clear silicone directly from tube onto surface. Press item to silicone. Set time is 15-20 minutes. Allow 24 hours for clear silicone to completely dry.

•Craft Glue

Craft glue is thick and all-purpose. It holds lightweight objects in place, is water-soluble, flexible, and dries quickly and clear. Craft glue is great for applying to smooth wood surfaces. Allow glue to dry thoroughly.

•Découpage Glue

Découpage glue is a glue, sealer, and finish all-in-one. It can be used as a sealer for wood, paper, prints, acrylic paint, and stains. It can be used as a glue for paper, fabric, and other porous materials. It is available in a gloss, matte, or antique finish. It is quick-drying, dries clear, and can be sanded to a smooth finish. It cleans up easily while wet with soap and water. It is non-toxic and waterbased.

Using an old paintbrush, paint back of artwork with glue.

Place artwork piece to be découpaged onto project surface. Press down with fingertips to remove any air bubbles.

Brush several light coats of glue over artwork. Let dry between coats.

•Reverse Découpage Glue

Reverse découpage glue creates a mosaic collaged look on glass or plastic ware using cards, paper napkins, gift wrap paper, ribbons, and silk flowers that are adhered from the back (or inside if using a vase).

•Glue Guns and Glue Sticks

Glue guns are trigger fed for even flow. They are lightweight and compact, with an electronic heating unit.

There are high temperature, dual temperature, and low temperature glue guns.

They come in a variety of sizes: standard, mini, and micro mini. They also use round or oval shape glue sticks. Note: *Be certain to purchase glue size, shape, and temp glue sticks compatible with glue gun.*

High temperature guns (380°F) use high temperature hot melt glue sticks. High temp glues are easy to use, bond quickly and dry in seconds.

Dual temperature guns use both low melt and high melt glue sticks.

Low temperature (225°F) guns use low temp melt glue sticks. Low temperature glues dry in up to 1 minute, allowing for repositioning of glued parts.

Low temperature glue guns and low temp melt glue sticks bond everything hot glue guns and high melt glue sticks do. They are safer than high temperature glues. They reduce risk of finger burns.

Glue sticks are available in clear (dries clear), cloudy (dries nearly invisible), or glitter sticks (decorative purposes). There are wood glue sticks (great for baskets, wreaths, minature doll furniture, leather, fabric, and multi-purpose home repair), super strength glue sticks (bonds glass to glass, metal to glass and allows 3-5 minutes working time before final bonding), high performance glue sticks (great for floral/craft projects), and jewelry glue sticks (great for metals, glass, plastics, shells, and beads), floral glue sticks (great for dried flowers, silks, and wreaths).

Note: When used in hot glue guns, the glue is very hot. Use tweezers or needlenose pliers to hold small objects in place. For larger objects, use a craft stick or pencil to apply pressure until glue is hard.

Strings of glue will be present. When glue cools it lifts right off surface.

•Rubber Cement

This glue allows wrinkle free pasting and is re-attachable. It is good for use on large surfaces and for mounting. Rubber cement is toxic.

•Spray Adhesive

This glue adheres to painted or unpainted surfaces for a permanent or temporary bond. It dries quickly and is water resistant.

Use spray adhesive for mounting objects and covering surfaces with fabric, flowers, or paper. It can be used on foil, foam, fabric, paper, glass, metal, yarn – virtually any surface.

Spray adhesive is flammable and toxic. Use only in well-ventilated area.

Paint Mediums
•Acrylic Medium

Acrylic medium produces a variety of textural effects. It can be used alone or mixed with acrylic colors and mediums.

•Antique Medium

Antique medium gives an old-fashioned, aged look to new paint.

Apply by rubbing over project surfaces with a clean cloth or paintbrush. Wipe off any excess. Allow to dry thoroughly.

•Crackle Medium

Using acrylic paint, apply basecoat to project using a flat or round brush. Allow basecoat to dry thoroughly.

Using an old flat or round brush, apply one coat of crackle medium using long sweeping strokes; thin coat for small cracks, thick coat for large cracks. *Note: Topcoat will crack in direction crackle medium is painted on.* Allow crackle medium to dry thoroughly.

Apply a topcoat of contrasting color acrylic paint using a flat or round brush or a sponge. *Note: Topcoat must be applied for cracking to occur.*

•Crystal Lacquer

Crystal lacquer creates 3-dimensional effects to any image.

Apply crystal lacquer to areas to raise. Do not apply to areas next to each other so wet edges touch each other. Allow 10-20 minutes to dry. Apply more on top until desired 3-dimensional effect is achieved.

•Pantina Green

Pantina green is used to create an antique green finish on copper, brass, or bronze.

To apply, brush Pantina Green on with a stiff bristle brush until a dull film appears. Allow to air dry.

•Photo Transfer Medium

This medium easily transfers black and white or color copies of cards, snapshots, and other prints to any paper, fabric, or wood project. Clear formula is used on white fabrics. Opaque formula is used on colored fabrics. Both are machine washable, waterbased, and non-toxic.

Have color copy made of object. If object contains words, reverse copy.

Apply photo transfer medium to color copy. Place color copy face down on project.

Using wet sponge, saturate paper of color copy in a circular motion. Remove all paper from color copy, leaving image on project. Let project dry thoroughly.

•Resin

Casting resin is a clear polymer finish/liquid plastic. There are different types of resin on the market.

Cards, photographs, prints, color copies, wrapping paper, stickers, or other items should have all edges flat and be completely sealed with 2-3 coats of découpage glue or acrylic spray sealer before resin is applied.

Wood surfaces should be completely sealed with a basecoat of acrylic gesso before resin is applied. If wood surfaces are not sealed thoroughly, air bubbles will appear and may not burst.

Prepare working surface. Work in well ventilated area.

Item being coated with resin should be elevated from protected working surface area several inches so excess resin may drip off. *Note: Edges of item(s) being coated with resin may be protected with masking tape.*

Measure ready-mix resin or one-to-one resin into unwaxed plastic cup.

Mix resin thoroughly.

Pour over entire surface as soon as mixed.

After pouring resin, air bubbles will rise and burst. Air bubbles are caused by resin degasing. Carbon dioxide is required for air bubbles to burst. Only exhale breathing on the surface or using a propane torch will cause air bubbles to burst.

On a small object, gentle exhale breathing on the surface will cause a few air bubbles to rise and disappear. A propane torch may be used for larger projects. Move torch side to side, six inches from surface. Manufacturer's suggest torching three times: (1) as soon as resin is poured, (2) ten minutes later, (3) fifteen minutes after second torching.

Use cardboard box to cover coated item to prevent dust from settling on surface during drying time.

Drips may be sanded off after overnight drying using fine-grit sandpaper.

Resin may be cleaned up using acetone.

Acrylic spray sealer may be used on project surface to help hide scratches.

•Snow Texture

This medium creates realistic dimensional effects such as snow, stucco, and terrain and adheres to all surfaces.

Apply snow texture with a brush, sponge, palette knife, or other tool. It may be thinned with water and may be tinted with acrylic paint. It dries hard in 2-3 hours. Snow texture cleans up with water.

Mitering Corners

Mitered corners have joining vertical and horizontal strips of fabric at a 45° angle to form a 90° corner.

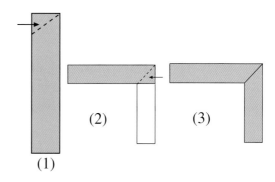

Lay first corner to be mitered, vertical side first, on project surface. Fold fabric under ¼" diagonally at 45° angle. See (1).

Using glue of choice, glue from corner to outside edge of fabric. Trim away excess fabric if needed

Repeat for three remaining corners. See (2) and (3).

Paint
•Acrylic Paint

Non-toxic acrylic paints have been used on projects in this book.

Acrylic paint cleans up with soap and water when wet, but it is always a good idea to use a drop cloth to protect work surfaces.

Always allow acrylic paints to dry thoroughly before applying additional coats or colors. When a quicker drying time is necessary, a blow dryer can be used to aid in drying the paint.

•Dimensional Fabric Paint

Creates a finished look and a 3-dimensional effect to project.

•Stained Glass Paint

Creates the look of stained glass on windows, mirrors, glass, and plexiglass.

Paintbrushes

Paintbrushes are the most common tool used for painting. Good quality synthetic brushes work best when using acrylic paints. Paintbrushes come in a variety of different sizes. The size of the brush will depend on the size of pattern being painted.

Brushes are numbered. This refers to the shape of the metal part of the brush that holds the bristles onto the shaft. The higher the number, the larger the brush.

Be certain to clean brushes thoroughly with soap and water until the water runs clean.

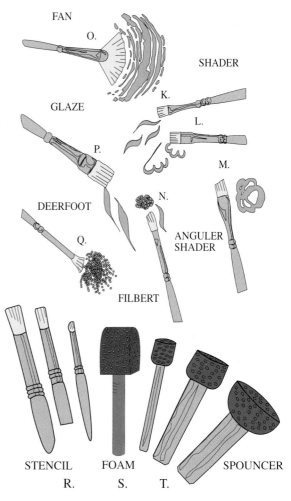

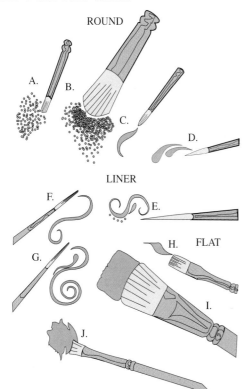

•Round

Round brushes have a fine point for delicate lines and detail work.

(A) Round Scrubber. Helps paint and fabric mediums permeate delicate fibers.

(B) Round Basecoater. Helps cover large areas quickly and easily.

(C) Fabric.

(D) Decorative.

•Liner

Liner brushes have a fine point and are good for delicate lines, detail work, lettering, and long continuous strokes.

(E) Decorative.

•Liner, Script

Script liner brushes are good for delicate lines and detail work. They hold more paint for long, continuous strokes.

(F) Decorative.

(G) Fabric.

•Flat

Flat brushes have longer hairs and a chisel edge for stroke work. They are good for filling in, blending, and wide sweeping strokes.

(H) Decorative.

(I) Flat Basecoater. The large size bristles are for precise coverage of large areas.

(J) Flat Scrubber. Helps paint and fabric mediums smoothly permeate fibers.

•Shader

Shader brushes have short hairs. They retain their chisel edge and are good for controlled stroke work and blending.

(K) Fabric.

(L) Decorative.

•Angular Shader

Angular shader brushes are good for stroke work and blending. They are good for painting flower petals.

(M) Decorative.

•Filbert

Filbert brushes have rounded tips that spread to desired width with pressure. They are good for stroke work, blending, and reaching tight corners of work.

(N) Decorative.

•Fan

Fan brushes are good for painting animal's whiskers, leaves, and foliage.

(O) Decorative.

•Glaze

Glaze brushes have long fibers. They are good for basecoating, filling in large areas, and applying finishes.

(P) Decorative.

•Deerfoot

Deerfoot brushes have round, angular, stiff bristles. They are good for painting foliage and texture on animals, and for stippling.

(Q) Decorative.

•Stencil

(R) Stencil brushes have densely packed, natural fibers for smooth, soft blends. They are good for use on fabric and hard surfaces. Sizes ¼" to 1" width.

•Foam

(S) Foam brushes are available in 1", 2", and 3"-wide brushes. They are good for coverage of large areas.

•Spouncer

(T) These sponge brushes come in ¾" to 1¾" width sponges. They are good for pouncing, stippling, or swirling. They can be re-used when wet.

Painting Techniques

Painting techniques used on projects in this book are as follows:

•Acrylic Gesso

A sealer, acrylic gesso, should be used before applying acrylic paint or resin. Use acrylic gesso as it comes from the jar.

Apply acrylic gesso to papier mâché surfaces before acrylic paint or resin is applied.

Sand all wood surfaces using fine-grit sandpaper. Remove sanding dust with a tack cloth. Apply acrylic gesso to wood surfaces before acrylic paint or resin is applied.

•Basecoat

In most cases, the project requires the entire surface to be painted.

Apply acrylic paint to all surfaces for full coverage.

Cover the area with two to three smooth, even coats of paint. *Note: It is better to apply several thin coats of paint, rather than one heavy coat.*

•Comma Stroke

Using a round brush, create a dot, rotate, and decrease pressure to create the tail of a comma or tear.

•Dimensional Paint

Using acrylic paint, place small amount of paint on brush. Scrape brush from top to bottom along tip of artwork to outline edge. This will deposit a bead of paint. This gives a more finished, antique look to artwork.

Using fabric paint, place paint applicator tip directly to artwork surface. Gently squeeze bottle to create 3-dimensional look to edge of artwork. Allow paint to dry thoroughly.

•Dots

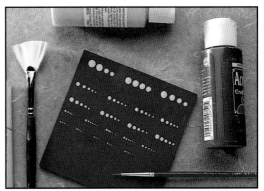

Dots are done by using a round object (end of paintbrush, stylus, corsage pin, or similar round tool).

Load tool, then dot on project until dots become smaller and smaller. Small dots are created by using a liner brush and rolling it to a point.

Cleaning and reloading the dotter between dots will assure the dots remain round and uniform.

•Dry-brush

Using an old flat brush, dip in a small amount of acrylic paint.

Remove excess paint from brush by working in criss-cross motion on paper towel.

Using a criss-cross motion, brush project with little to no pressure to create a soft texture.

•Float

Floating is used to apply shading and highlighting.

Dampen the largest flat brush that will accommodate the area to float.

Wipe excess water on paper towel.

Load one corner of brush, up to ⅓ of width, of chisel edge of bristles with paint. Stroke the brush back and forth on a palette to work the paint into the bristles and soften the color.

Apply brush to painting surface. The paint color should appear darkest at the loaded corner and gradually fade to clear water on opposite corner.

Note: If paint spreads all the way across chisel edge of bristles, rinse brush and reload.

•Marbleize

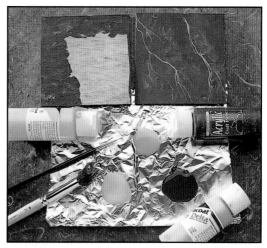

Basecoat project surface by loading flat or round brush with three to four different colors, blending slightly using one color as dominant color.

To make veins, dip paintbrush into one-part water and one-part paint. Pick a point on edge of project and lay brush down. Pull brush along surface with a twisting, turning motion, making a vein. The twisting motion varies the thickness, and the turning makes a crooked, natural looking line. Some parts of the vein should have more paint than others. Veins in marble are much like the branches of a tree – irregular, splitting, and often forming a Y-shape.

Repeat using a small, round liner paintbrush to make smaller veins.

•Outline

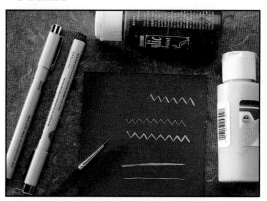

Note: If using a permanent marker to outline, seal the artwork by applying a light coat of acrylic spray sealer before outlining with permanent marker.

Outlining is done after patterns have been traced, transferred, and filled in with color.

Go back and paint fine outline lines, retracing if necessary. Painters with a great deal of experience will opt to detail using a fine liner brush. Painters with little or no experience will opt to use a fine- or medium-point permanent marker.

When using a liner brush, load paint thinned with water. Pull the brush through the paint, turning to get a fine point. Hold the brush perpendicular to the work and line the desired areas. The thickness of the line will be determined by the amount of pressure applied to the brush.

•Rubber Stamp

Cover entire rubber stamp with pigment ink. Stamp on project.

Sprinkle embossing powder over stamped area. Remove excess embossing powder. Heat with embossing heat gun.

For more detailed instructions, see directions provided in comprehensive rubber stamping publications.

•Splatter

Using an old toothbrush, dip bristles of toothbrush into paint that has been slightly diluted with water.

Hold toothbrush about 6 to 8 inches away with bristles pointed toward the project. Draw a finger or thumb across bristles causing the paint to spatter onto project.

•Sponge

Load the top of sponge with paint.

Blot sponge on paper towel until most of paint has been removed.

Apply the paint to project by lightly "blotting" the sponge up and down, using heavy or light coverage as desired.

•Stipple

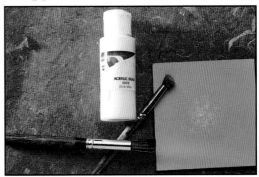

Stipple painting is repeated small touches using an old brush or cosmetic sponge. Load a brush or sponge with very little paint. Bounce brush or sponge tip on paper towel then apply lightly to project. Vary dot sizes to create shadow or texture effect.

•Swirl

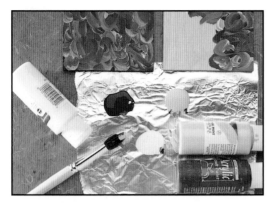

Place small amount of each paint on aluminum foil.

Dip flat or round brush in each color. Swirl slightly on project with brush, building up paint to add texture. Do not swirl too much or colors will mix together, forming a gray/brown color. Let paint dry thoroughly.

•Wash

Washing refers to the application of acrylic paint to a surface for transparent coverage.

Mix one-part paint and three-parts water. Apply this paint wash to sealed wood using an old flat brush. Several coats of light wash produce a soft, but deep, transparent color.

Allow wash to dry thoroughly between coats.

•Watercolor

Note: If using acrylic paint, dilute acrylic paint to watercolor paint consistency with water.

Dip flat brush in water then remove excess water from brush by blotting on a paper towel.

Apply slightly darker color of paint to side of brush and blend, staying on track until paint fades evenly across brush. The paint will fade from dark to light.

Using a fine-tip round brush, gently blend paint to soften edges. More water may be used if necessary to soften edges.

•Apply Sealer

The final step in Painting Techniques is applying an acrylic spray or brush-on sealer to set the paint and protect the artwork.

Apply several light coats of sealer to entire project. Let sealer dry.

Sandpaper

Sandpaper comes in many grades. Use coarse paper for rough shaping, medium for moderate sanding, and fine for finish sanding. Follow manufacturer's instructions.

Soldering

It is recommended that a face mask be used while soldering to avoid breathing toxic fumes.

If this is the first time using a soldering iron, practice on scraps. A little solder goes a long way. If a mistake is made, touch the iron to the solder. The heat will melt the solder again and allow removal of it.

Wrap copper foil tape around all glass edges.

Using an old paintbrush, apply flux over copper foil tape. Using old rag, wipe excess flux off glass.

Using soldering iron, solder around glass edges until desired look is achieved. Build up areas or make edges smooth or bumpy.

The soldering spot can be covered up with a variety of metallic paints that will blend with the metal almost perfectly. Soldering may cause metal to tarnish. If this occurs, use fine steel wool to gently clean the tarnished spot.

Sponges

Sponges are used when sponge painting. They are found in many different sizes and textures.

Be certain to clean sponges thoroughly after use with soap and water until the water runs clean.

Tracing & Graphite Paper

Tracing paper is thin enough to see through and allows original pattern lines to be retraced easily.

Graphite paper is coated on one side. When it is pressed by a pencil, it transfers the graphite or chalk to the surface under it.

Transferring the Pattern

If directions indicate enlarging pattern, place pattern in a photocopy machine. Set the machine to percentage required and enlarge.

Two methods of transferring pattern are given. Choose the method that is most comfortable and convenient.

•Method One

The photocopy of pattern can be traced onto tracing paper and transferred onto the item using graphite paper.

Position carefully and tape graphite paper between pattern and item with graphite side facing item. Firmly, trace the pattern using a pencil. Lift corner slightly and make sure the pattern is transferring.

•Method Two

The photocopy of pattern can be traced onto and cut from a manila envelope or mylar.

Position carefully and tape cut out pattern on item. Carefully trace around pattern using a pencil, or if necessary, a ballpoint pen.

Remove the pattern once the design has been transferred.

Woodworking

Some projects in this book require a jigsaw, miter saw, scroll saw, table saw, or any type of saw that can cut through thicker pieces of wood.

Ribbon & Stitch Diagrams

Boat Leaf

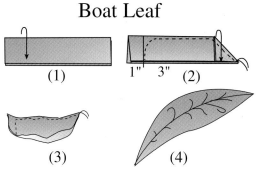

(1)   (2)

1" 3"

(3)   (4)

Fold an 8" length of ribbon in half crosswise. See (1).

Measuring in from raw edges, mark 1" for stem length. See (2).

Sew a gathering stitch inverting leaf. See (3).

Draw in the gathers. Knot thread and cut. Do not cut excess ribbon. Open leaf and shape for completed Boat Leaf. See (4).

Fabric Rose

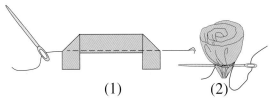

(1)   (2)

Fold 2" x 25" fabric strip in half lengthwise with long, raw edges aligned. Fold fabric ends at right angles leaving ½" allowance. Stitch running thread on long raw edge; leaving needle and thread attached. See (1).

Gather fabric slightly while wrapping to make flower. Force needle through lower fabric edge. See (2) for completed Fabric Rose. Secure thread. Do not trim excess. Fluff rose.

Five-Petal Flower

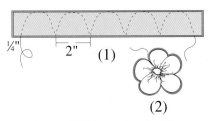

¼"   2"   (1)

(2)

Using 10½" length of ribbon, leaving ¼" allowance at each end, divide ribbon into five sections by folding. Mark the outer edge. Sew a continuous stitch. See (1).

Pull gathers tightly to form flower center. Backstitch and knot; leaving needle and thread attached. Direct needle back through beginning knot. Pull tight until knots touch. Hold ribbon together, backstitch, and knot. Cut thread. Completed Five-Petal Flower. See (2).

Folded Leaf

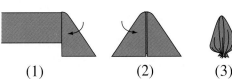

(1)   (2)   (3)

18

Cut ribbon into 2½" lengths. Fold ends of ribbon forward diagonally. See (1) and (2).

Gather across bottom edge of folds using floral wire for a completed Folded Leaf. See (3).

Herringbone Stitch

B C   A

Work stitch from right to left. Bring needle up at A and down at B.

Bring needle up at C, taking a small horizontal backstitch.

Continue working, alternating from side to side.

Running Stitch

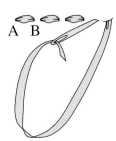

A B

Work a line of straight stitches with an unstitched area between each stitch. Come up at A and go down at B.

To End Stitching

Secure stitches in place before beginning new area. Do not drag ribbon from one area to another. Tie a slip knot on wrong side of ribbon work to secure stitch in place and end ribbon.

Ribbon can be tacked into place with small amount of hot glue.

Tuft

Fold each 4" length of ribbon in half.

Secure bottom of tuft by twisting wire around bottom edge.

Fray raw edges for completed Tuft.

Your projects do not need to be identical to the ones featured in this book.

Select cards to match your home or desired occasion.

The three tile boards displayed here (instructions on page 78) show that just a change of cards and color scheme can make every

project a one of a kind work of art.

Even instruction steps can be added or subtracted to produce a totally new result.

For example, the resin sealing step was omitted from the tile board on the right to create a different look.

These examples show the versatility of design ideas and occasions that each set of instructions may be used for.

With just a snippet of imagination,

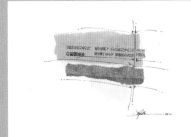

handmade greeting
cards can be created
by recycling your
greeting cards and
other traditional
items that are often
thrown away –

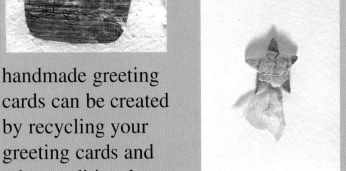

for example:
pieces of art
paper, moss,
clay, ribbon,
broken bits
of costume
jewelry.

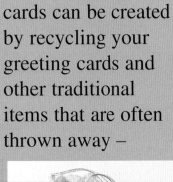

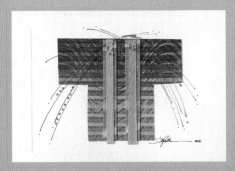

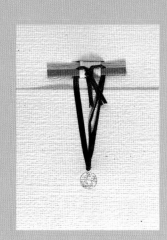

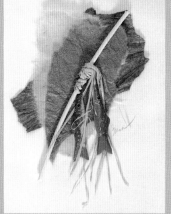

It is
r
e
a
l
l
y
that
easy!

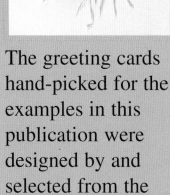

The greeting cards
hand-picked for the
examples in this
publication were
designed by and
selected from the
leading greeting
card companies.

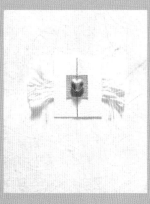

With this book, you
can use any card you
desire, with any set of
instructions, with any
project you choose.

Here for your
inspiration
are examples
of handmade
cards created
by some of the
leading card
designers.

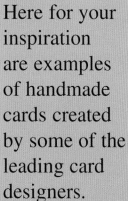

January

Hearts Desire

2

3

I resolve somehow to be a brighter, stronger

person starting now.

1

be me
a feather
some jelly-sweet bread
rain on the roof
and a bright,
brassy bed
a big purple hat
apple that's red,
and a kiss every night
on the top of my head!

4

Celestial Insights

1
Recall When

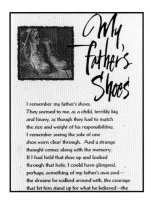

Materials

Acrylic spray sealer
Card: with artwork that can be separated from saying
Cardboard: lightweight, 5" x 7"
Embellishments: (2)
Frame: 5½" x 7½"
Glue: craft
Knife: craft
Masking tape
Netting: ¼ yd.
Paint: acrylic
Paintbrush
Paper: handmade, 5" x 7"
Ribbon: ⅝"-wide, wire-edged, ½ yd.
Scissors: paper edgers
Staple gun and staples

How To

✳Refer to General Inst. on pgs. 6-18.

1. Remove glass from frame. Using acrylic paint, wash frame. Apply spray sealer to frame.

2. Using craft knife, cut out artwork from card. Using paper edgers, trim edges of artwork and edges of card where artwork was cut out.

3. Place handmade paper behind card, filling cut out section of card. Place paper and card into frame and secure.

4. Place glass into frame. Lay card over glass, paper over card, and cardboard over paper. Secure into frame. Place embellishments on top of glass, slightly under frame edges to secure.

5. *Note: Netting tears easily.* Cover entire frame with netting. Using masking tape, secure netting to back of frame.

6. Using craft glue, place and glue artwork on top of netting over space where artwork was cut from card.

7. Tie a bow in center of ribbon. Using staple gun and staples, staple ends of ribbon to corners on top back of frame.

In Other Words

Use a card pertaining to childhood memories. Embellishments could include a lock of hair or piece of jewelry.

2
Picture Perfect

Materials

Acrylic spray sealer
Card
Charms: (4)
Frame: 6⅝" x 8⅝" with opening 5½" x 3½"
Glue: craft
Knife: craft

Picture Perfect continued

Paint: acrylic;
    watercolors
Paintbrushes
Pantina green
Paper: watercolor, coarse,
    5½" x 3½"; hand-
    made, 8⅝" x 1½"
Pen: calligraphy
Sponge

How To

✳Refer to General Inst.
    on pgs. 6-18.

1. Place card on top
of glass allowing ¾" of
card to extend onto side
edge of frame. Using
craft knife, cut card that
is on side edge of frame.
Set aside.

2. Using acrylic
paint, sponge frame.
Apply spray sealer.

3. Tear piece of
handmade paper to go
under side edge of cut
card.

4. Using craft glue,
glue handmade paper to
side edge of frame. Glue
larger portion of card
onto top of glass. Glue
cut off card on top of
paper, 1⁄16" away from
inside edge of frame,
matching edge of picture
on glass.

5. Wet coarse
watercolor paper and
streak on watercolors to

match card. Place paper
under glass inside frame.

6. Using calligraphy
pen, write desired saying
on bottom of paper.

7. Apply pantina
green over charms.

8. Glue charms on
opposite bottom corner
of frame that handmade
paper and card are
glued to.

In Other Words

Purchase cards and
charms while traveling
and frame these
memories of the times
spent in faraway places.

3
Memory Pillows

Materials

Color copy of cards: (2)
    (if cards contain
    words, reverse copy)
Fabric: plain, light color
    16½" square (2)
Needles: hand-sewing
Photo transfer medium
Pillow forms: 16½"
    square (2)
Ribbons: ⅜"-wide,
    1 yd.; ⅝"-wide,
    1 yd.; 1⅜"-wide,
    1½ yds.
Scissors: craft
Sewing machine
Sponge
Thread: clear nylon

How To

✳Refer to General Inst.
    on pgs. 6-18.

1. Apply photo
transfer medium to color

copy of cards. Place cards face down on coordinating fabric.

2. Using ribbon, fabric of choice, and thread for invisible stitches, machine-stitch around pictures. Intermix ribbon and fabric for special contrast around picture.

3. With right sides together, machine-stitch front and back of pillows together, leaving opening on one edge to insert pillow form. Turn right side out and insert pillow forms. Stitch opening closed.

In Other Words

Pillows can be made any size from tiny sachets to large bed pillows.

4
Memories Saved

Materials

Book with blank pages:
    9¼" x 9"
Card
Charms
Glue: craft
Paintbrush
Pantina green
Paper: handmade,
    8" x 9"; 10¼" x 6"
Pen: calligraphy
Scissors: craft

How To

✳Refer to General Inst. on pgs. 6-18.

1. Using craft glue, place and glue 8" x 9" handmade paper diagonally across front cover of book. Tear and glue 10¼" x 6" handmade paper to cover portion of 8" x 9" handmade paper.

2. Wrap paper around back binding of book, and fold piece over top edge of book to inside

front cover. Glue to secure.

3. Using craft scissors, cut out artwork from card. Glue artwork over 8" x 9" paper on lower right corner of book.

4. Using paintbrush and pantina green, apply over charms to antique. Glue charms on front of book as desired.

5. Using calligraphy pen, write saying on 8" x 9" handmade paper.

In Other Words

Scrapbooks can be made to save anything from private thoughts to favorite recipes to much loved photographs. Match the card to the subject.

This card could be the cover for a journal of favorite wines and their labels.

5

6

7

5
Recipe Book

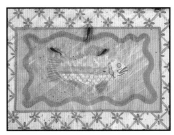

Materials

Book with blank pages:
   9" x 5¾"
Card
Card stock: (2 sheets)
Chop sticks: (1 set)
Glue: craft
Pen: fine-point
   permanent

How To

✳Refer to General Inst.
  on pgs. 6-18.

1. Using craft glue, cover front and back of book with card stock.

2. Glue decorative die-cut card, or cut out artwork from card, on front of book.

3. Refer to "Recipe" Pattern if doing a Japanese cook book. Using pen, write Recipe in Japanese on front of book, or substitute words in the language of the country the food originates from.

4. Glue chopsticks onto front of book.

"Recipe" Pattern
Enlarge 260%

本の料理の本

In Other Words

A recipe book filled with tea and pastry recipes and pictures of tea parties would make a wonderful shower present.

6
Fridge Notepad

Materials

Card: 4" x 11"
Knife: craft
Magnet sheet: 5" x 8"
Notepad: 3" x 5"
Pen
Scissors: craft

How To

✳Refer to General Inst.
  on pgs. 6-18.

1. Using craft scissors, cut out artwork from card with 3" x 5" bottom section for note pad. *Note: If card does not have 3" x 5" bottom section, use lightweight cardboard.*

2. Using pen, trace card pattern on back of magnet sheet.

Fridge Notepad continued

3. Using craft scissors, cut out traced pattern from magnet.

4. Remove paper backing from magnet. Apply sticky side of magnet to back of card.

5. Center notepad on 3" x 5" bottom section of card. Using craft knife, slit where top of notepad will be placed. Insert notepad cardboard back through slit.

In Other Words

Individual notepads can be left on the fridge so the intended receiver will know immediately which should be read by whom.

7
Pear Plate

Materials

Acrylic spray sealer
Card
Foam brush
Glue: découpage
Gold leaf adhesive
Knife: craft
Paint: acrylic (2-4)
Paintbrush
Plate: glass, clear
Silver leafing
Sponge
Varnish: clear

How To

✳Refer to General Inst. on pgs. 6-18.

1. Clean plate. Using craft knife, cut out artwork from card.

2. Using découpage glue on front side of artwork, découpage artwork to back inside bottom circle of plate. Let dry overnight.

3. Using foam brush, apply gold leaf adhesive to back of plate. Allow to set one hour.

4. Using silver leafing, break apart and rub onto gold leaf adhesive.

5. Apply a light coat of acrylic spray sealer onto back of plate.

6. Using acrylic paint and sponge, sponge desired colors randomly onto back of plate. Basecoat back of plate using three different colors of paint, letting each coat dry thoroughly.

7. Using varnish, seal back of plate. Apply several coats.

In Other Words

HALLOWEEN
I shudder with fright
On this ghost filled night.
And shield my eyes from the awful sight,
Where owls and cats and broad winged bats,
Are mingled with witches in tall crowned hats.

Make sets of plates to serve for each individual holiday.

February

I will love you always.

1
Angel Box

Materials

Box: papier mâché
  5¾" x 7¾", with cut
  out lid 3¾" x 5¾"
Card
Glue: adhesive &
  sealant; gloss
  découpage
Paint: acrylic
Paintbrush
Plexiglass: 5½" x 7½"
Varnish: gloss
Wrapping paper

How To

✴Refer to General Inst.
  on pgs. 6-18.

1. Using acrylic paint,
marbleize outside top of
box lid. Paint design
around edges of box lid.
Apply varnish to outside
top of box lid.

2. Using découpage
glue, découpage

wrapping paper around
outside of box.

3. Remove cardboard
piece from inside frame
box lid.

4. Using adhesive &
sealant glue, glue glass
inside lid. Place card
artwork face down onto
glass, centered inside
3¾" x 5¾" cut out in
frame. Glue cardboard
piece inside lid to secure
artwork and glass.

2
Valentine Clock

Materials

Acrylic gesso
Acrylic spray sealer
Cards: (2-4)
Clock workings
Finial: 2"
Glue: craft; découpage
Hearts: 1¼", wooden (4)
  or desired shape
Jigsaw
Paint: acrylic
Paintbrushes
Pencil
Sandpaper: medium-grit
Scissors: craft

Spray paint: gold
Tracing & graphite paper
Wood: ¾"-1"-thick pine,
  12" x 18"

How To

✴Refer to General Inst.
  on pgs. 6-18.

*Note: Any pattern for
clock can be cut to match
theme of cards being
used or occasion being
given.*

1. Transfer Clock
Base Pattern and Heart
Pattern to wood. Using
jigsaw, cut out patterns
from wood. Determine
placement for and cut
hole in clock base to
accommodate clock
workings. Sand cut out
patterns.

2. Using craft glue,
glue finial to top of
clock. Glue one heart to
lower right and one heart
to left bottom side of
clock.

3. Apply acrylic
gesso to wood surfaces.

4. Using acrylic
paint, basecoat clock and
hearts.

5. Using craft
scissors, cut out artwork
from cards.

6. Using découpage
glue, place and
découpage artwork onto
front of clock. Let glue

dry thoroughly. Sand front of clock.

7. Using acrylic paint, comma stroke and place descending dots on clock. Paint finial as desired.

8. Using craft glue, glue four 1¼" hearts onto clock at 12:00, 3:00, 6:00, and 9:00 positions.

9. Lightly spray front of clock with spray paint.

10. Apply acrylic spray sealer.

11. Add clock workings, according to manufacturer's instructions.

Heart Pattern
Enlarge 220%

Cut 2

Clock Base Pattern
Enlarge 220%

3
Photo Album

Materials

Binder: 3-ring
Card
Foam board: 3" x 5"
Glue: découpage
Knife: craft
Marker: permanent
Paintbrush
Paper: decorative,
    12" x 12";
    translucent, Japanese,
    24" x 36"
Pencil
Scissors: craft
Sponge: small

How To

❋Refer to General Inst. on pgs. 6-18.

1. Using craft scissors, cut out artwork from card.

2. Dilute découpage glue 1:1 ratio with water. Apply glue to binder cover.

3. Apply translucent paper to binder cover and gently press with damp sponge.

4. Let project dry thoroughly. Repeat process once more.

5. Using craft knife, cut design to correspond to artwork from foam board, if desired.

6 Apply glue to foam board. Wrap foam board with small piece of decorative paper.

7. Using pencil, write saying on scrap piece of decorative paper. Using desired color of permanent marker, write saying.

8. Glue decorative pieces and artwork to binder cover.

In Other Words

4
All Occasion Frame

Materials

Card
Drill with ¹⁄₁₆" bit
Flowers: assortment, dried; paper; silk
Glue: craft; hot glue gun and glue sticks
Hanger: ¾" brass, screw-in
Leaves: small, silk; velvet
Paint: acrylic, metallic gold
Paintbrush
Paper: decorative, 3" square
Ribbon: ⅛"-wide, satin, 2"
Ring: 2¾" wooden, stained
Scissors: craft
Sponge: small
Toothbrush

How To

❋Refer to General Inst. on pgs. 6-18.

1. Using outside edge of ring as pattern, trace circle around card artwork to be framed.

2. Using craft scissors, cut out traced pattern. Cut out small individual flower artwork from card.

3. Using drill, drill hole in top of ring. Screw in brass hanger.

4. Using gold acrylic paint, sponge lightly over wooden ring.

5. Using gold acrylic paint, dimensional paint a thin, fine line around edge of flower artwork.

6. Using craft glue, place small bead around outside edge of artwork to frame. Glue ring onto artwork. Let set for 10 minutes.

7. Using metallic gold paint, splatter frame and artwork.

8. Using hot glue gun and glue stick, hot-glue flowers and leaves as desired to frame.

9. Using decorative paper, cut out slightly larger circle than wooden ring and glue to back of wooden ring.

In Other Words

A joyous Christmas

Frame a picture for a family and add their name and address, or frame a new baby picture and add name, date, etc.

February

6

The

ornaments

of a house

are the

friends who

frequent it.

Ralph
Waldo
Emerson

A true friend is a pearl
who reads your deepest
needs and so spares
you the shame of giving
your heart's desires
a name.
Jean de la Fontaine

5
Small Candy Jar

Materials

Card
Embellishments
Glue: reverse découpage
Jar: small, glass with lid
Paint: acrylic; glass (2)
Paintbrushes
Ribbon: ½"-wide, sheer
⅔ yd.
Scissors: craft

How To

✳Refer to General Inst.
on pgs. 6-18.

1. Using craft
scissors, cut out four
pieces of artwork from
card.

2. Using découpage
glue, découpage artwork
to inside of jar following
manufacturer's
instructions.

3. Using acrylic
paint, basecoat around
artwork on outside of jar
and around edge of lid in
a checkered pattern.

4. Using ribbon, tie
a bow around neck of jar.

5. Embellish top of
jar lid as desired
(ceramic button on
project model).

In Other Words

Small jars can be
used as favors at
wedding showers or
holiday parties.

6
Oriental Ball

Materials

Ball: 3" Styrofoam
Bell cap: ¾" gold
filigree
Cards: (2-3)
Charms: gold filigree,
butterfly wings
(2 pair)
Cotton swabs: (2-3)
Glue: craft; hot glue gun
and glue sticks
Knife: craft
Paper punch: ¼"
decorative, flower
shape
Pencil
Scissors: craft
Tassel: 3"
Wire: beading, 1½ yd.

How To

✳Refer to General Inst.
on pgs. 6-18.

1. Using decorative
paper punch, punch out
shapes from cards.

2. Using craft glue,
apply glue to Styrofoam
ball, working small areas
at a time.

3. Using damp cotton
swab to pick up shapes,
apply shapes to glued
area on Styrofoam ball.
Continue to apply glue
and shapes, working
small areas, on
Styrofoam ball until
entire surface is covered.
Slightly overlap shapes
to give appearance of
"scales."

4. Using craft scissors, cut wing charms apart into four separate pieces.

5. Using pencil, mark four equidistant 1" lines toward top one-third of ball for wing placement.

6. Using craft knife, cut slits on four 1" lines. Apply glue to raw edge on each wing area and glue wing into slit.

7. Cut beading wire into four 10" lengths. Thread each length of beading wire through top part of each wing. Twist to secure wire. Bring ends of wire together and form into a loop. Wrap loop with more wire to secure loop.

8. Using hot glue gun and glue stick, hot-glue bell cap to bottom center of ball. Hot-glue tassel to bead cap.

In Other Words

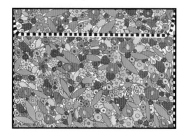

Ornaments will look completely different when made from cards with pastel colors or those that have metallic accents.

7
Ornate Finial

Materials

Acrylic gesso
Beads: 8mm round; pre-strung
Braid: ¼ yd.
Cards: (2)
Finials: wooden, curtain (2)
Glue: craft; hot glue gun and glue sticks; wood
Paint: acrylic, gold
Paintbrushes
Scissors: craft
Straight pins
Tape measure
Thread: thick, ¼ yd.
Trims: ⅜"-wide, ¼ yd.; ¾"-wide, ½ yd.

How To

✳Refer to General Inst. on pgs. 6-18.

1. Using wood glue, attach curtain finials together to form ornament.

2. Apply gesso to ornament. Using acrylic paint, basecoat ornament.

3. Cut out artwork from cards to fit desired sections of ornament.

4. Using craft glue, glue artwork to ornament.

5. Using gold acrylic paint, dry-brush ornament for antique appearance.

6. Tie thread into a loop. Push straight pin through loop and into top of ornament for hanger.

7. Cut trims to fit around desired sections of ornament. Using hot glue gun and glue stick, hot-glue trims around ornament. Hot-glue pre-strung beads around ornament. Hot-glue braid around center of ornament. Hot-glue round bead to bottom tip of ornament.

In Other Words

Finials can be used not only for Christmas ornaments but for curtain tie backs, lamp or shade pulls, or decorative home accents.

March

The coming of love is like the coming of Spring - the date is not to be reckoned by the calendar.
It may be slow and gradual; it may be quick and sudden.
But in the morning, when we wake and recognize a change in the world without, blossoms on the sward, warmth in the sunshine, music in the air, we say Spring has come.

Edward George Bulwer Lytton

1
Shadow Box

Materials

Acrylic gesso
Acrylic spray sealer
Brads: ¾" metal (4)
Cards: (2)
Clamps: large (4)
Chisel
Embellishments
Glass: ⅛" thick, 12¾"
  x 10½"
Glue: adhesive & sealant;
  clear silicone; wood
Hinges: (2)
Magnets: ¾" diameter (2)
Paint: acrylic (2)
Paintbrush
Pencil
Router
Sandpaper: coarse-grit;
  medium-grit
Scissors: craft
Table saw
Wood: ¼"-thick plywood,
  13" x 12½"; ¾"-thick
  plywood, 9" x 18";
  block, 1" square

How To

✳Refer to General Inst.
on pgs. 6-18.

1. Using table saw,
cut two 1½" x 12½"
pieces for shadow box
sides, two 1½" x 11"
pieces for shadow box
sides, and one 11" x 12½"
piece for shadow box
back, from ¼" plywood.

2. Using clamps and
wood glue, glue sides
and back of shadow box
together. Check to make
certain all pieces are
squared. Let glue dry
thoroughly. Using
medium-grit sandpaper,
sand all edges of box.

3. Cut two 3" x 18"
and two 3" x 16" pieces
from ¾" plywood for
frame. Miter corners at
45° angle.

4. Using clamps and
wood glue, glue frame
pieces together. Check to
make certain all pieces
are squared.

5. Using router, cut
¼"-wide x ⁵⁄₁₆"- deep
groove around inside
edge of frame for glass
placement. Using a
chisel, remove round
corners.

6. Apply acrylic
gesso to shadow box and
frame. Using acrylic
paint, basecoat inside and
outside of shadow box

with light color acrylic
paint. Basecoat frame
with slightly darker color
acrylic paint.

7. Using coarse-grit
sandpaper, sand painted
surfaces for antique
appearance.

8. Apply spray sealer
to painted surfaces.

9. Attach shadow
box to frame with hinges.

10. Place and secure
glass in frame using one
brad in each corner of
frame.

11. Glue one side of
magnetic catch to frame.
Glue other side of
magnetic catch to 1"
square wood block. Glue
block to box side with
magnet side up, touching
magnet on frame.

12. Using craft
scissors, cut out artwork
from one card and
rectangular shape
from one card. Add
3-dimensional
appearance to artwork
by rolling the edges
over a pencil.

13. Using adhesive &
sealant and clear silicone
glue, embellish inside of
shadow box as desired.

March

2

3

They say there is a fairy in each streaked tulip.
I have rows and rows of them beside my door.
by Amy Lowell

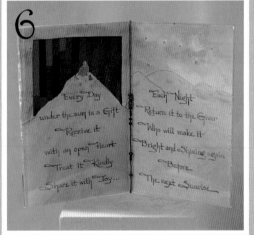

6

Every Day
under the sun is a Gift
Receive it
with an open Heart
Treat it Kindly
Share it with Joy...

Each Night
Return it to the Giver
Who will make It
Bright and Shining again
Before
The next Sunrise

I wonder if on
a rainy night,
the sandman
sends the
mudman.

George Carlin

5

4

2
Special Moments

At the heart and soul of marriage is a love that is nourished by everyday things.

Materials

Box frame: 3½" x 5"
Cards: (2)
Charms
Fabric: ½ yd.
Glue: clear silicone; craft
Knife: craft
Masking tape
Paintbrush
Paper: handmade, scrap
Scissors: craft

How To

✳Refer to General Inst. on pgs. 6-18.

1. Using coordinating fabric and craft glue, cover frame.

2. Using craft scissors, cut back of card off one card. Cut out artwork from second card.

3. Using craft knife, cut card to fit frame opening.

4. Using clear silicone, glue glass inside frame. Using masking tape, secure card onto glass.

5. Tear two pieces of handmade paper to go under raised artwork on front of box. Using craft glue, glue paper to front of box.

6. Using clear silicone for 3-dimensional appearance, attach artwork around glass on front of box.

7. Add charms as desired.

In Other Words

A special moments frame is an easy gift to make to celebrate a special occasion.

Add a photograph in place of the second card.

3
Garden View

Materials

Cards: duplicate for box, heavy-weight (4); artwork scene
Embellishments
Glue: clear silicone; craft
Knife: craft
Wood: ¼"-thick balsa, 4" x 4½"

How To

✳Refer to General Inst. on pgs. 6-18.

1. Using craft glue, glue two cards together to form box.

2. Using craft knife, cut one card 5½" x 4½". On 5½" edge, fold in ½" from edge and glue to inside of box for bottom.

3. Cut card 6¼" x 4½" for lid. Fold in ½" and glue to top of outside of back of box. Fold 1½" in from other end and tuck inside to form lid of box.

4. Glue balsa wood to inside bottom of box for support.

5. Cut out desired artwork scene from card.

6. Using clear silicone, attach artwork to front of box as desired.

7. Embellish front of box as desired.

In Other Words

Card boxes can be made for that very special gift whether it be ring size or large enough to hold a treasured porcelain figurine.

4
Letter House

Materials

Acrylic gesso
Acrylic spray sealer
Box: papier mâché, house-shape, 4½" x 5½"
Card: house scene
Glue: craft
Markers: permanent; watercolor (3)
Paint: acrylic
Paintbrushes
Pencil
Sponge: ½" x ¼"

How To

✳Refer to General Inst. on pgs. 6-18.

1. Apply gesso to papier mâché inside and outside of box.

2. Using acrylic paint, basecoat inside and base of box.

3. Using craft glue, glue card onto front and sides of box.

4. Basecoat back and eaves of box using vertical strokes to resemble wood siding. Basecoat roof lid to resemble shingles. Using sponge, randomly add small brick marks to chimney.

5. Using watercolor markers, detail six dormer windows.

6. Using acrylic paint, stipple climbing rose to left side of house. Stipple additional flowers on climbing rose.

7. Using permanent marker, edge bottom base of house.

8. Apply spray sealer to entire house.

In Other Words

Do not forget a letter house can be a farm house, Victorian mansion or French country cottage, seasonal such as a haunted Halloween castle, or a Christmas southern plantation.

5
Stamp Box

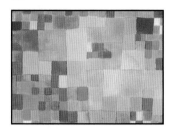

Materials

Acrylic gesso
Acrylic spray sealer
Card: to match Letter
    House
Glue: craft
Knife: craft
Knob: wooden ball, 1"
Marker
Paint: acrylic
Paintbrush
Sandpaper: fine-grit
Stamp box: wooden,
    with lid, 1¾" x 2"

How To

✳Refer to General Inst.
    on pgs. 6-18.

1. Using sandpaper,
lightly sand inside and
outside of stamp box.

2. Apply acrylic
gesso to outside of stamp
box, lid, and knob.

3. Using craft knife,
cut out artwork from card
to fit around stamp box.

Additional small detail
pieces can be cut out and
applied over artwork.

4. Using acrylic
paint, basecoat outside of
stamp box, lid, and knob.

5. Using craft glue,
glue artwork and small
detail pieces around
outside of stamp box.
Glue knob on top of lid.

6. Using marker,
draw around lid rim.

7. Apply spray sealer
to stamp box, lid, and
knob.

6
Quilt Frame

Materials

Beads: variety of
    sizes (12)
Cards: (2)
Frame: double photo
    plexiglass, 6" x 8"
Knife: craft

Overdyed thread:
    (1 strand)
Pen: calligraphy
Quilted fabric piece

How To

✳Refer to General Inst.
    on pgs. 6-18.

1. Using craft knife,
cut backs off of both
cards. Cut out a portion
of one card to place
fabric quilt piece.

2. Using calligraphy
pen, write desired saying
onto each half, or one
half, of card. Slide each
half of card into each
side of frame.

3. Cut quilted fabric
piece to fit opening in
first card. Slide quilt in
back of first card.

4. Place beads onto
overdyed thread. Wrap
thread over frame in
center of double frames.
Tie thread in back of
double frame.

In Other Words

March

On the first real warm
day, you can sit on the
back steps in your PJs
before church, drink
coffee, study the back
yard which was such a
dump a week ago, but
with tulips coming on
strong and a faint green
haze on the lilacs, a
person can see this
is not the moon, but
Earth.

Garrison Keillor

7
Envelope Card

Materials

Card
Envelope: with border
   (3)
Glue: découpage
Knife: craft
Paper: handmade, 5½"
   square
Scissors: craft; paper
   edgers

How To

✳Refer to General Inst.
  on pgs. 6-18.

1. Using craft knife,
cut out artwork from
card.

2. Using paper
edgers, cut out handmade
paper in rectangle shape
to fit in center of card
and slightly over side
borders.

3. Using craft
scissors, cut top flap off
one envelope. Cut away
flap from second
envelope, leaving ½".

4. Lay envelopes,
right sides down, on
work surface. Glue ½"
flap inside first envelope.

5. Using cut out
flaps, cut out border and
glue down inside center
fold.

6. On front of card,
glue handmade paper in
center. Glue artwork
from card over handmade
paper toward center of
card. Fold card in half.
Write message inside.

8
Charm Picture

Materials

Card
Charms
Clamps: (2)
Cording: elastic, ¾ yd.
Drill with ⅛" bit
Glue: craft; industrial-
   strength
Marker: erasable
Paper: handmade, scrap;
   tissue, scrap
Plexiglass:
   5" x 7" (2)
Ribbon: coordinating
Scissors: craft

How To

✳Refer to General Inst.
  on pgs. 6-18.

1. Using craft glue,
glue coordinating design
(handmade paper, tissue
paper, ribbon) onto
selected card. Center
card on one piece of
plexiglass. Place
remaining piece of
plexiglass on top of
card.

2. Using clamps,
secure plexiglass pieces
together.

3. Mark desired
location, for elastic
cording, with marker.
Drill holes through both
pieces of plexiglass.

4. Using craft
scissors, cut cording into
equal lengths. Thread
cording through drilled
holes and tightly knot on
back of plexiglass.
Remove clamps.

5. Using industrial-
strength glue, glue
charms in desired
location on front of
plexiglass.

3

2

4

1
Heart Necklace

Materials

Acrylic gesso
Acrylic spray sealer
Beads: silver, ¼" (2);
⅜" (2); ½" (2)
Card
Cording: silk, ¹⁄₁₆", 1 yd.
Glue: craft; découpage
Heart: wooden,
2⅓" x 1½"
Knife: craft
Paint: acrylic
Paintbrush
Scissors: craft

How To

✳Refer to General Inst.
on pgs. 6-18.

1. Apply acrylic
gesso to wooden heart.
Using acrylic paint,
basecoat heart.

2. Using craft knife,
cut out artwork from
card.

3. Using découpage
glue, découpage card
design onto heart. Let
dry. Apply spray sealer.

4. Using craft knife,
cut out small notches at
top curve of heart.

5. Using craft
scissors, cut cording in
half. Knot one end of
each piece, leaving ½"
tail. Fray tail.

6. Using silver
beads, thread three beads
on each piece of cording,
largest bead on the
bottom, smallest bead on
top. Knot cording after
last bead.

7. Using craft glue,
glue knot to notched area
of heart allowing frayed
ends to show in front of
heart.

8. Measure cording
to desired length and
knot together. Trim ends.

In Other Words

Matching bracelets
can be made as easily as
the necklace.

2
Envelope Sachet

Materials

Cards: (2-3)
Cord: gold
Envelope: decorative
Glue: craft; hot glue gun
and glue sticks
Leaves: ¾" rose (5)
Paint: acrylic
Paintbrush
Paper: tissue, decorative,
6" square; lace
edging, decorative
Pencil
Potpourri
Ribbons: ⅛"-wide, ½ yd.;
¾"-wide ombre, wire-
edged, ⅓ yd.
Scissors: craft
Tracing paper
Tulle: 2" square (2)

How To

✳Refer to General Inst.
on pgs. 6-18.

1. Transfer Envelope
Pattern onto tracing
paper. Lift all flaps on

decorative envelope and flatten. Using pencil, trace pattern onto decorative envelope.

2. Using craft scissors, cut out pattern from decorative envelope. Bend envelope on dotted lines.

3. Using craft glue, glue paper lace edging to top and bottom flap. Glue ⅛"-wide ribbon around raw edges of side and bottom flaps. Fold envelope on dotted lines and glue sides in and bottom flap up.

4. Using craft scissors, cut out artwork from card. Using acrylic paint, dimensional paint along tip of artwork.

5. Using hot glue gun and glue stick, run thin bead along three outside edges of tulle. Press two edges together forming a pouch. Stuff

with potpourri. Seal top edge of pouch using hot glue.

6. Gather ¾"-wide wire-edged ribbon to fit around cut out artwork. Hot-glue ribbon to back edge of artwork. Hot-glue leaves to artwork.

7. Hot-glue artwork and ribbon to top part of potpourri pouch.

8. Tie bow using gold cord. Hot-glue bow to front of artwork.

9. Tuck decorative tissue paper between envelope flap and potpourri pouch.

In Other Words

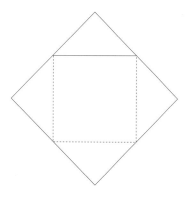

Envelopes can be made to hold things other than sachet. Use to give a friend a sentimental letter or a family member a treasured photograph.

3 Switch-plate

Materials

Acrylic gesso
Card
Glue: découpage
Knife: craft
Paint: acrylic (5)
Paintbrush
Resin: high gloss
Ruler
Scissors: craft
Switchplate cover: wood, single-switch

How To

✳Refer to General Inst. on pgs. 6-18.

1. Apply acrylic gesso to switchplate cover.

2. Using acrylic paint, basecoat, then

Envelope Pattern
Enlarge 280%

watercolor outside edges of switchplate cover.

3. Measure and cut card to fit top of cover. Glue card to cover.

4. Using a craft knife, cut out screw holes and switch hole.

5. Apply resin onto switchplate cover following manufacturer's instructions.

In Other Words

Switchplates can become a major accent in a room by simply using a little imagination. Have a switchplate cut oversized or in an unusual shape, add charms, or make cut-outs.

4 Garden Scene

Materials

Cards: one with border; one with artwork for center piece
Fabric: ⅛ yd.
Flowerpot: clay, 1½"
Flowers: dried, small
Frame: 4½" x 6½", or to fit card
Garden rake: miniature, 4" tall
Glue: craft; rubber cement
Hand saw
Knife: craft
Lace: ⅔ yd.
Paintbrush
Scissors: craft
Stickers
Spanish moss

How To

✳Refer to General Inst. on pgs. 6-18.

1. Using hand saw, cut clay pot in half lengthwise.

2. Using craft knife, cut center from border card.

3. Using rubber cement, glue border card over floral card. Using craft scissors, trim edges of card if needed.

4. Using craft glue, glue rake and flowerpot to front of card.

5. Glue flowers into flowerpot.

6. Attach stickers to front of card as desired.

7. Cut fabric in four pieces for each side of frame, with ½" extra added for each side.

8. Using paintbrush and craft glue, wrap and glue fabric to frame, vertical sides first, mitering corners. Wrap all fabric around back of frame and glue to secure.

9. Glue lace around frame, mitering corners.

10. Place embellished card into frame and secure.

April

If I could command the shining of the Spring,
could grasp it without putting it out,
I should wish to send it to that beautiful person
at the border of Heaven. Li T'ai-po

5
Card Mat

Materials

Card
Frame: 8" x 10"
Glue: découpage
Knife: craft
Mat board: 12" x 9"
Paint: watercolor (3-5)
Paintbrush
Pencil
Scissors: craft

How To

✳Refer to General Inst. on pgs. 6-18.

1. Using craft knife, cut away inside of card leaving any part of artwork from card and entire border around card.

2. Using découpage glue, glue card to one corner of mat board. Let glue dry thoroughly. Cut mat board around exact pattern of card.

3. Center matted card on top of remaining 7" x 9" mat board.

4. Using pencil, trace around inside pattern of matted card. Cut mat board along traced pattern.

5. Using watercolor paint, watercolor 7" x 9" mat board to coordinate with card.

6. Glue matted card to 7" x 9" watercolored mat board. Place in frame with desired picture and secure.

In Other Words

Mats can be made to frame special photographs, a much loved verse, an antique piece of jewelry, or to show a sense of humor.

6
Watering Can

Materials

Acrylic gesso
Acrylic spray sealer
Cards: (2-3)
Charms: (5)
Glue: découpage; hot glue gun and glue sticks; wood
Paint: acrylic (2)
Paintbrush
Pencil
Ribbons: sheer, (2 colors), 1 yd. each
Sandpaper: medium-grit
Scissors: craft
Scroll saw
Toothbrush
Tracing & graphite paper
Watering can: purchased 8¼", or see Watering Can Patterns
Wood: ¾"-thick pine, scrap; ¼"-thick pine, 8" x 12"

Watering Can continued

How To

✳Refer to General Inst. on pgs. 6-18.

1. Referring to Watering Can Patterns below, transfer and cut 12 Slats, one Base, and one Base with hole from ¼" wood. Transfer and cut one Handle and one Spout from ¾" wood.

2. Using scroll saw cut out patterns.

3. Using sandpaper, sand all pieces.

4. Apply acrylic gesso to all pieces. Using acrylic paint, basecoat all pieces. Splatter all pieces with contrasting color of acrylic paint.

5. Using wood glue, glue spout to one slat. Glue handle to one slat. Glue slats, straight end down, to base without

hole ¼" apart. *Note: Slat with handle and slat with spout should be across from each other.*

6. Glue base with hole approximately 1" down from tops on inside of slats.

7. Transfer slat pattern to cards. Using craft scissors, cut out twelve patterns from cards.

8. Using découpage glue, découpage card patterns to outside of slats. Let glue dry thoroughly. Apply thin coat of découpage glue to entire project.

9. Apply spray sealer to entire project.

10. Using hot glue gun and glue stick, hot-glue charms to slats as desired.

11. Using ribbons, tie bow on handle.

In Other Words

Watering cans may be filled with something other than flowers. Try candy in the kitchen, cotton balls in the bath, or paper covered pencils in the study.

7 Watering Can Flowers

Materials

Buttons: decorative (5)
Fabric: 2" x 25" (5) for roses
Florist picks: wooden, green with wire attached, 2½" (41)
Glue: hot glue gun and glue sticks
Needle: hand-sewing
Ribbon: ⅛"-wide wire-edged, 10½" (5) for flowers; ⅛"-wide wire-edged, green, 8" (9) for leaves
Scissors: craft
Thread: coordinating
Wire
Wire cutters

Watering Can Patterns
Enlarge 280%

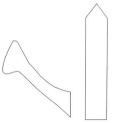  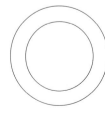

Spout	Slat	Handle	Base
Cut 1	Cut 12	Cut 1	Cut 1 with hole Cut 1 without hole

How To

⁂Refer to General Inst. on pgs. 6-18.

1. Refer to Fabric Rose Diagram on pg. 18. Using five fabric strips, make five Fabric Rose(s). Set aside.

2. Refer to Five-Petal Flower Diagram on pg. 18. Using five 10½" pieces of wire-edged ribbon, make five Five-Petal Flower(s). Set aside.

3. Refer to Boat Leaf Diagram on pg. 17. Using craft scissors, cut nine 8" lengths of ⅞"-wide green ribbon for leaves. Make nine Boat Leaves. Set aside.

4. Using wire on picks, wrap three picks together for fabric rose stems. Repeat for a total of five stems. Wrap two picks together for a total of fourteen stems for boat leaves and five-petal flower stems.

5. Using hot glue gun and glue stick, wrap and hot-glue fabric and ribbon allowance around flat side of pick. Using wire, wrap tightly around fabric and ribbon to secure.

6. Hot-glue one decorative button onto center of each five-petal flower.

8
Bird House Trio

Materials

Acrylic gesso
Bird houses: purchased, or handmade (3)
Card: large enough to cover 3 houses (banner or tri-fold)
Dowels: ¼" x 2" (3) for perch
Drill: with ¼" and 1" bits
Glue: découpage
Hammer
Knife: craft
Nails: small, finishing (10)
Paint: acrylic (8-10)
Paintbrushes
Pencil
Ruler
Sandpaper: medium-grit
Saw: miter
Scissors: craft
Wood: ¾"-thick pine, 4" x 8" (3) for houses; ⅜"-thick pine, 2" x 5½" (3) for base; ⅜"-thick pine, 1¼" x 6" (6) for roof.

How To

⁂Refer to General Inst. on pgs. 6-18.

1. Transfer Bird House Pattern onto wood. Using miter saw, cut out pattern pieces. Cut each roof piece at 30° angle.

2. Center and measure 4" from bottom of house front and mark for door hole placement. Center and measure 2⅟₁₆" from bottom of house front and mark for perch placement. Using drill and 1" bit, drill door hole through house. Using ¼" bit, drill ½" deep hole for perch.

3. Sand front of house and front edges of roof where cards will be découpaged onto house.

4. Tightly match top corners of roof pieces and nail to house. Center

51

Bird House Trio continued

house along back edge of base and nail in place. Repeat for other two houses.

5. Apply acrylic gesso to all wood pieces.

6. Using acrylic paint, watercolor front of each house. Wash each roof and perch. Dilute three colors of paint and paint each base in a plaid pattern.

7. Using craft scissors and ruler, measure and cut card to fit front of each house.

8. Using découpage glue, découpage card to front of each house, extending portions of card to edges of roof.

9. Using craft knife, cut card from door hole and perch hole on front of each house.

10. Using wood glue, glue dowels in drilled perch holes.

11. Apply thin coat of découpage glue over cards on front of house and along roof edges.

In Other Words

**Bird House Pattern
Enlarge 280%**

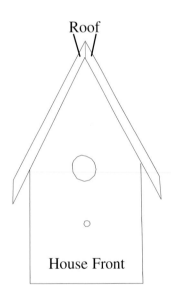

Cut 3 House Fronts
Cut 3 Roofs (each side)

Other shapes can be covered for accents in home decor. Why not try using one long rectangle across the top of a window or an angel topper over the door to welcome holiday guests.

May

Let all the joys be as the month of
May, and all thy days
be as a wedding day.

Francis Quarles

May is green as no other,
May is much sun through small leaves,
May is soft earth, and apple blossoms,
And windows open to the south wind.
May is full light wind to lilac.

Amy Lowell

1
Heart Sachet

Materials

Beads: ⅛" round (6);
   seed, ¼" (3)
Card
Flowers: ⅜" roses,
   porcelain (3)
Glue: craft; hot glue gun
   and glue sticks
Needle: thin, crewel;
   hand-sewing
Ribbon: silk, 3/16"-wide,
   1 yd.; silk, ¼"-wide,
   ¼ yd; chiffon, 3"-
   wide, 1⅜ yds.
Scissors: craft
Thread: coordinating

How To

✳Refer to General Inst.
  on pgs. 6-18.

1. Using craft
scissors, cut back off of
card. Set back of card
aside.

2. Using craft
scissors, cut ¼"-wide
ribbon into 8" lengths.
Thread crewel needle
with 8" length of ribbon.
Knot one end of ribbon.
Pierce hole for ribbon on
front side of card for
each stitch. Stitch over
ribbon areas on card.
Ribbon may be secured
with tiny bead of hot
glue.

3. Using 3/16"-wide
ribbon and running stitch,
stitch around front of
card ½" from edge.

4. Using
coordinating thread and
hand-sewing needle, sew
beads on in groups of
three.

5. Using hot glue
gun and glue stick, hot-
glue porcelain roses onto
front of card.

6. Using craft glue,
apply thin line of glue
around edges of card.
Glue front and back of
card together, leave top
and inside of card open.

7. Cut 3"-wide
ribbon in half and any
leftover ¼"-wide ribbon
in half. Knot ribbons
together at one end. Hot-
glue knot to top left side
corner of card. Repeat
with remaining ribbon
for opposite side of card.
Tie ends of ribbon into
bow. Trim ends of
ribbon.

8. Fill and hang as
desired.

In Other Words

Fill your sachet with
confetti and hand it to
wedding guests to wish
the bride and groom
goodbye.

2
Stationary Holder

Materials

Card
Glue: craft; spray
   adhesive
Knife: craft
Paper: card stock,
   4" x 6"; decorative;
   heavy-weight,
   10" x 24";

Ribbon: 1"-wide sheer,
  ¾ yd.
Ruler
Scissors: craft; paper
  edgers

How To

✳Refer to General Inst.
  on pgs. 6-18.

1. Using craft
scissors, cut one
Stationary Holder Pattern
from heavy weight, 10" x
24" paper.

2. Fold (A) at dotted
line over (B), right sides
together. Fold (C) at
dotted line, right side
facing wrong side of (A).

Fold and tuck tabs into
pocket formed by (A)
and (B). Fold folder in
half vertically.

3. Cut decorative
paper to fit outside of
folder and to cover inside
pockets. Apply spray
adhesive and adhere
decorative paper to
folder. Trim any excess
paper.

4. Cut two 1"-wide
slits, ¼" apart, on vertical
fold to thread ribbon
through.

5. Using Stamp
Envelope Pattern, make
one envelope using
lightweight paper. Using

craft glue, glue to inside
of folder onto pocket.

6. Cut back off of
card. Cut out desired
saying or design from
card for note card. Using
paper edgers, cut
coordinating card stock
slightly larger than note
card for backing. Trim
edges of note card with
paper edgers.

7. Center and glue
note card to backing.
Punch hole in top of
backing. Thread ribbon
through slit in folder and
hole in note card. Tie
bow with ribbon to close
folder.

Stationary Holder Pattern
Enlarge 200%

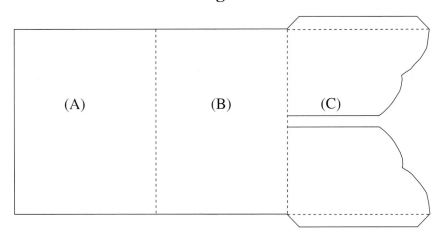

(A) (B) (C)

Stamp Envelope
Pattern
Enlarge 280%

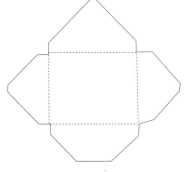

3
Tussy Mussy

Materials

Cards: (2)
Charm
Glue: craft; hot glue gun and glue sticks
Lace: 2"-wide, ⅔ yd.
Leaves: velvet, (2-3)
Needle: hand-sewing
Paint: acrylic
Ribbon: ¾"-wide wire-edged, 12"; 1"-wide wire-edged, ½ yd.; 2"-wide wire-edged, 1 yd.
Rubber bands
Scissors: craft
Tape: floral
Thread: white
Trim: ¼"-wide decorative braid, 5"
Wire: floral, 6" length for each flower
Wire cutters

How To

❋Refer to General Inst. on pgs. 6-18.

1. Using craft scissors, cut artwork from one card.

2. Using wire cutters, cut wire into 6" lengths for stems for each piece of artwork and tuft used. Cover each length of wire with floral tape.

3. Cut 1"-wide wire-edged ribbon into 2½" lengths for each Folded Leaf (seven used in this project). Attach each leaf to a stem.

4. Cut 2"-wide wire-edged ribbon into 4" lengths for each Tuft (six used in this project). Attach each tuft to a stem.

5. Using hot-glue gun and glue stick, hot-glue artwork to remaining stems. Hot-glue folded leaves at edge of artwork backs.

6. Using 12" of ¾"-wide ribbon, tie into a bow. Secure bow with floral wire.

7. Gather length of lace at top edge to 5-6" for ruffle. Using needle and thread, join and secure ruffle, leaving 2½" diameter opening.

8. Using second card, roll cone shape 4" long, with 2½" opening at top of cone. Using craft glue, glue cone. Secure cone toward top and middle with rubber bands until glue is dry. Cut ½" off cone bottom tip, leaving small opening. Remove rubber bands.

9. Arrange artwork stems, tuft stems, and velvet leaves, placing larger artwork to the back, working forward with smaller artwork. Wrap arrangement securely with floral tape, forming one large arrangement stem.

10. Using hot glue gun and glue stick, hot-glue trim over seam edge of cone, leaving excess at bottom end.

11. Hot-glue ruffle to upper inside edge of cone allowing lace to spill over edge.

12. Insert arrangement in ruffle inside cone. Using wire cutters, trim exposed wrapped wire from end of arrangement stem.

13. Remove arrangement. Place drop of hot glue into cone tip. Insert arrangement into cone to secure.

14. Wrap trim over tip of cone and hot-glue at back of cone.

15. Hot-glue charm and bow on front of cone.

May

4

WITH SYMPATHY
In the Loss
of Your
Grandmother

Although at times of sorrow
there's so little words can say,
Still may these words
of sympathy
help comfort you today.

How could I forget you, Grandmother, it was you who gave me my first taste of homemade ice cream. You watched smiling as I ate too much, and then you kissed me sweetly, not even minding my sticky little face. Every summer, you filled my room with fresh cut roses taken from your prized bushes. You calmed me as I fretted at what I saw as the waste of their tender blossoms. It was you who taught me that even though cut roses die, the joy they bring lasts forever in our memory. Each night you pulled me up in your lap and rocked me gently before the fire. You sang to me songs your grandmother sang to you. In gentle whispers, you shared stories of your youth. Now I have children of my own and though you can not be here, I share with them all I learned from you. My ice cream will never be as sweet, nor my roses as fragrant, but the songs I sing and the stories I tell bring back the lessons you helped me learn. Nothing you did was ever wasted, Grandmother, for the joy you brought me I give to others, and you will live in all of us forever.

Ginger Mikkelsen

4
Memory Frame

Materials

Acrylic gesso
Brads: ¾" metal (4)
Card
Clamps: large (4)
Chisel
Crackle medium
Embellishments
Glass: ⅛" thick, 12¾"
    x 10½"
Glue: découpage, antique
    finish; hot glue gun
    and glue sticks; wood
Hinges: (2)
Magnets: ¾" diameter
    (2)
Paint: acrylic (2)
Paintbrush
Paper: wrapping
Pencil
Router
Sandpaper: medium-grit
Scissors: craft
Stain: fruitwood
Table saw
Wood: ¼"-thick plywood,
    13" x 12½"; ¾"-thick
    plywood, 9" x 18";
    block, 1" square

How To

✳Refer to General Inst.
   on pgs. 6-18.

1. Using table saw, cut two 1½" x 12½" pieces for shadow box sides, two 1½" x 10" pieces for shadow box sides, and one 11" x 12½" piece for shadow box back, from ¼" plywood.

2. Using clamps and wood glue, glue sides and back of shadow box together. Check to make certain all pieces are squared. Let glue dry thoroughly. Using medium-grit sandpaper, sand all edges of box.

3. Cut two 2" x 16" and two 2" x 14" pieces from ¾" plywood for frame. Miter corners at 45° angle.

4. Using clamps and wood glue, glue frame pieces together. Check to make certain all pieces are squared.

5. Using router, cut ¼"-wide x ⁵⁄₁₆"-deep groove around inside edge of frame for glass placement. Using a chisel, remove round corners.

6. Using craft scissors, cut wrapping paper to fit inside shadow box back.

7. Apply acrylic

gesso to inside of shadow box and frame.

8. Using acrylic paint, basecoat inside of shadow box and frame.

9. Apply crackle medium to frame. Using acrylic paint, apply topcoat, in contrasting color, to frame.

10. Apply stain to inside of shadow box and frame.

11. Sand all edges of frame for antique appearance.

12. Using antique finish découpage glue, découpage wrapping paper to inside shadow box back.

13. Attach shadow box to frame with hinges.

14. Place and secure glass in frame using one brad in each corner of frame.

15. Using wood glue, glue one side of magnetic catch to frame. Glue other side of magnetic catch to 1" square wood block. Glue block to box side with magnet side up, touching magnet on frame.

16. Using craft scissors, cut front from card. Trim card as desired. Using hot glue gun and glue stick, embellish shadow box as desired.

May

5

6

7

*Wait not for
Spring to
pass away,
Love's
Summer
months
begin with
May!*

Oliver Wendell Holmes

5
Heart Card

Use these easy-to-make cards to give daily to yourself, a child, or a friend with a motivational or inspirational sentiment tucked inside.

Materials

Card
Pencil
Scissors: craft
Tracing paper

How To

❋Refer to General Inst. on pgs. 6-18.

1. Transfer Heart Card Pattern onto tracing paper. Using pencil, trace pattern onto card.

2. Using craft scissors, cut out pattern from card. Bend card on dotted lines.

Heart Card Pattern
Enlarge 240%

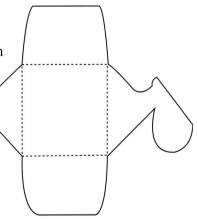

6
Pansy Pin

Materials

Cards: (2)
Foam board: paper-covered, 5" x 7"
Gemstone: ⅛"
Glue: adhesive & sealant; craft
Knife: craft
Leaves: ¾" rose (8)
Scissors: craft
Paint: acrylic
Paintbrush
Pin back: 1-1¼"
Wire cutters

How To

❋Refer to General Inst. on pgs. 6-18.

1. Using craft knife, cut out one 1" x 2" rectangle from foam board for base of pansy pin. Cut out six to eight ¼" squares from foam board to separate flowers and give pin 3-dimensional effect.

2. Using craft scissors, cut out artwork from cards.

3. Using acrylic paint, basecoat two coats to back of each artwork piece and ¼" squares of foam board. Allow paint to dry thoroughly.

4. Using acrylic paint, dimensional paint along tip of artwork for a finished, antique look.

5. Using adhesive & sealant glue, arrange and glue artwork pieces to each other, building forward by sandwiching ¼" square foam board pieces between artwork fronts and backs to make arrangement.

6. Glue arrangement onto 1" x 2" rectangle foam board base.

7. Using wire cutters, cut wire stems from leaves. Using craft glue, glue leaf base to artwork backs.

8. Glue gemstone to artwork. Glue pin back onto back of foam board base.

In Other Words

7
Floral Scene

Materials

Beads: seed (21)
Cards: duplicate (2); one to be framed
Charms: leaf (6)
Finials: wooden, 1" x 2" (3)
Glue: adhesive & sealant; clear silicone
Granite stone textural medium
Paintbrush
Pencil
Picture frame: plexiglass, 5" x 7"
Scissors: craft
Wood: ½"-thick balsa, 1" x 9" (2)

How To

✳Refer to General Inst. on pgs. 6-18.

1. Using craft scissors, cut out artwork from one card.

2. Cut out duplicate artwork from second card. Bend artwork by rolling over pencil. This creates a 3-dimensional look to artwork. For added 3-dimensional look to artwork, cut around some petals leaving the center solid and bend petals by rolling over pencil.

3. Using adhesive & sealant, glue artwork around edges of plexiglass frame.

4. Using clear silicone, apply to the back of each piece of duplicate artwork and place on top of first cut artwork.

5. Using beads and charms, embellish front of frame as desired.

6. Place third card inside frame.

7. Using adhesive & sealant, evenly space and glue finials beginning in center of one piece of balsa wood. Glue remaining piece of balsa wood on top of finials to form decorative wall.

8. Apply stone texture to wall, following manufacturer's instructions.

9. Glue frame onto top of wall.

June

There is a glory in tree and
blossom, a thrill in the wild
birds
tone,
a balm
in the
Summer
breezes,
that love
revealeth
alone.

B. S. Parker

1
Lamp Shade

Materials

Cards: (5-6)
Charms: (3)
Drill with ⅛" bit
Glue: découpage
Lamp shade
Needle: embroidery;
    hand-sewing
Paintbrush
Paper: handmade,
    8" x 24"
Ribbons: 1"-wide, sheer,
    4 yds. (2)
Scissors: craft
Thread: gold

How To

✳Refer to General Inst.
  on pgs. 6-18.

1. Using découpage
glue, découpage
handmade paper to lamp
shade.

2. Using craft
scissors, cut out artwork
from cards. Découpage
artwork to lamp shade.

Overlap some pictures,
varying sizes.

3. Using hand-
sewing needle and
thread, add decorative
stitches around artwork.

4. Drill ⅛" holes 1½"
apart around top and
bottom of lamp shade.

5. Using embroidery
needle and two shades of
ribbon, stitch through
pre-drilled holes, leaving
two long tails to tie bow
on top of lamp shade.

6. Using thread, tie
charms as desired
between ribbon tails.

7. Tie bow with long
tails on top of lamp
shade.

2
Woven Book Mark

Materials

Cards: one to cut
    weaving strips; one
    small enclosure card

or gift tag; one card
    for artwork
Fabric: 12" square
Foam board: 8" x 9¼"
Frame: 10¾" x 9½"
Glue: craft
Leaves: ¾" satin (3)
Marker: extra-fine tip,
    metallic, permanent
Paint: acrylic
Paintbrush
Pencil
Ribbons: ⅛"-wide, ¼ yd.
    (5); ¾"-wide
    grosgrain, ½ yd.;
    ¾"-wide wire-edged,
    ombre, ¼ yd.;
    1½"-wide metallic,
    ¼ yd.
Ruler
Scissors: craft
Tape: double-sided;
    masking

How To

✳Refer to General Inst.
  on pgs. 6-18.

1. Using craft
scissors, cut card for
weaving strips same
width as enclosure card
or gift tag.

2. Measure and mark
1" down from top edge
of card for weaving strips
with pencil. Measure and
mark intervals of ⅛", ¼",
and ½" weaving strips
across width of card.

3. Cut strips
beginning at bottom of
card up to 1" mark at top
of card.

4. Using ⅛"-wide ribbons, weave across strips, making one row of each color. Place 1½"-wide metallic ribbon at end of weaving placing one strip behind, one strip in front of ribbon until complete. Trim strips, leaving ½" at each edge.

5. Using acrylic paint, dimensional paint tips of weaving strips to outline edges.

6. Using craft glue, tuck and glue ribbon ends to back side of weaving to secure.

7. Bind and glue edges of enclosure card or gift tag using grosgrain ribbon.

8. Glue weaving to enclosure card or gift tag. Wrap ¾"-wide wire-edged ombre ribbon around joined edge, covering seam.

9. Cut out artwork from card.

10. Dimensional paint tips of artwork to outline edges.

11. Glue artwork at top left and right of bookmark.

12. Glue leaves onto weaving.

13. Using 12" square fabric and marker, write saying on fabric.

14. Stretch fabric over foam board. Using masking tape, secure fabric to back of foam board.

15. Place fabric into frame and secure.

16. Using double-sided tape, secure woven book mark onto fabric.

3
Suitcase Table

Materials

Balusters: wooden for legs (4), desired height

Cards, postcards, old money, tokens, and mementos

Drill with ¼" bit

Glass: rounded corners, cut to fit top of suitcase

Glue: craft

Saw

Screws: 1½" flat head wood (4)

Suitcase: old

How To

✳Refer to General Inst. on pgs. 6-18.

1. Using cards, postcards, old money, tokens, and mementos, determine placement on suitcase.

2. Using craft glue, glue cards, postcards, old money, tokens, and mementos on suitcase.

3. Using saw, cut balusters to desired leg height.

4. Drill four holes into each corner of suitcase and baluster ends for leg placement.

5. Attach legs to suitcase using screws.

6. Place glass on top of suitcase.

In Other Words

Suitcases can be made to hold dolls and doll clothes for that special little girl in your life.

June

I only know that the Summer sang in me. Edna St. Vincent Millay

4
Bridal Hanky Holder

Materials

Card
Card stock: 8½" x 11"
Embellishment
Fabric: to line folder,
   ⅓ yd.
Glue: craft; hot glue gun
   and glue sticks
Needle: crewel; hand-
   sewing
Paint: dimensional fabric
Pearls: 2mm (6); 6mm
   (3)
Ribbon: ½"-wide, 2 yds.;
   1¼"-wide wire-edged,
   ⅜ yd.
Scissors: craft
Trim: ½"-wide scalloped,
   ½ yd.

How To

✳Refer to General Inst.
   on pgs. 6-18.

1. Using craft
scissors, cut top edge

from card front exposing
upper back edge of card.

2. Using dimensional
fabric paint, dimensional
paint top edge of card
front.

3. Cut card stock
slightly smaller than
front and back of card.

4. Gather 12" length
of 1¼"-wide ribbon to fit
width of cut card front.

5. Using hot glue
gun and glue stick, hot-
glue gathered ribbon
between front card and
front card stock.

6. Hot-glue
scalloped trim at top
back edge and bottom
back edge of front card.

7. Punch holes in
card using needle over
ribbon areas on card.
Using crewel needle and
½"-wide ribbon, stitch
and hot-glue over ribbon
areas through punched
holes

8. Cut fabric slightly
smaller to fit inside back
folder. Using craft glue,
glue fabric onto inside
back folder. Glue back
card stock onto fabric
liner.

9. Glue ½"-wide
ribbon down inside fold
of folder. Glue trim along
front bottom edge and
back top and side.

10. Hot-glue pearls to
front of card.

11. Embellish front of
card as desired.

In Other Words

A hanky holder can
be made from silly cards
and given stuffed with
stockings or a tie.

5
Book Mark

Materials

Card with matching
   printed envelope
Glue: craft
Paper: handmade or
   embossed, size of
   card
Paper punch: ¼" round
Ribbon: ³⁄₁₆"-wide, ½ yd.;
   ¼"-wide grosgrain,
   1 yd.

Ruler
Scissors: craft

How To

✳Refer to General Inst. on pgs. 6-18.

1. Using craft scissors, cut off back from envelope and discard. Fold and miter edges of envelope 2¾" x 5¾" so printed side shows on back and front of bookmark.

2. Tear edges from paper. Center and glue card on top of paper.

3. Glue ³⁄₁₆"-wide ribbon over card edges, mitering corners. Glue ¼"-wide ribbon to back side of bookmark, mitering corners. Center and glue card to envelope.

4. Punch a hole in center top of bookmark. Loop remaining ¼"-wide ribbon in half. Thread looped end of ribbon through hole. Thread ribbon ends through loop and pull tight. Trim ends of ribbon.

5. Cut additional artwork from card to embellish as desired.

In Other Words

Book marks can be made to mark the last read page in bibles, children's books, cook books, etc.

6
Magnet
Teacups

Materials

Cards: die cut (2)
Crystal lacquer
Embellishments
Glue: découpage
Knife: craft
Magnet sheet: 10" x 5"
Pencil

How To

✳Refer to General Inst. on pgs. 6-18.

1. Using découpage glue, glue cards closed.

2. Place cards onto magnet sheet.

3. Using pencil, trace around artwork. Using craft knife, cut out artwork from magnet sheet.

4. Using découpage glue, glue magnets to back of artwork.

5. Apply crystal lacquer on desired areas of magnet to create 3-dimensional appearance, following manufacturer's instructions.

6. Embellish magnets as desired.

In Other Words

Make magnets for each member of the family!

June

8

O winding roads
that I know so
well, Every turn,
every hollow
and hill! They
are set in my
heart to a
pulsing tune
Gay as a honey-
bee humming in
June.

Amy Lowell

7

9

With my father, life became an adventure.
The minute he walked in the door at night
everything became charged, brighter, more
colorful, more exciting.

Victoria Segunda

7
Ship Frame

Materials

Acrylic gesso
Acrylic spray sealer
Cards: border; artwork
Frame: pine, 10" square
Glue: découpage
Knife: craft
Paint: acrylic (4)
Paintbrush
Paper towel
Picture hanger: 1¼"
   metal
Picture or photo

How To

✳Refer to General Inst.
   on pgs. 6-18.

1. Apply acrylic
gesso to frame.

2. Using acrylic
paint, basecoat frame.
Paint stripes on frame.
Gently wipe thin stripes
with damp paper towel.

3. Using craft knife,
cut out artwork from one
card. Cut out border from
second card into four
corner sections.

4. Using découpage
glue, découpage border
sections around corners
of frame opening.

5. Using acrylic
paint, basecoat space
between border sections.
Wash frame.

6. Découpage
artwork to frame as
desired.

7. Apply acrylic
spray sealer to frame.

8. Place desired
picture or photo in frame
and secure.

In Other Words

This is the perfect gift
for a summer home or
special decoration for the
holidays.

8
Cigar Box

Materials

Acrylic gesso
Acrylic spray sealer
Buttons: silver orb,
   1½"-wide (4)
Cards: (4-5)
Card stock
Cigar box: 7" x 8½"
Glue: craft; industrial-
   strength
Knife: craft
Markers: medium-point,
   permanent (2)
Paint: acrylic; oil pastel
   crayons (2)
Paintbrush
Paper towels
Photos: (1-2)
Plastic wrap
Stickers
Toothbrush

How To

✳Refer to General Inst.
   on pgs. 6-18.

1. Apply acrylic
gesso to inside and
outside of cigar box.

2. Using acrylic paint, basecoat outside of cigar box.

3. Using a square piece of plastic wrap crumpled into a ball, dip into acrylic paint and wipe excess onto paper towel. Randomly sponge onto top and sides of cigar box.

4. Using toothbrush, splatter top and sides of cigar box.

5. Refer to Diamond Pattern. Using card stock and craft knife, cut out pattern.

6. Using Diamond Pattern and oil pastel crayons, draw diamonds onto all four sides of cigar box. Brush off excess oil pastel.

7. Using marker, draw lines around diamond patterns. Repeat process with different color marker.

8. Arrange cards, photos, and stickers as desired onto cigar box. Using pencil, trace around each, then remove. Apply thin layer of craft glue to back side of cards and photos. Reposition onto cigar box lid. Attach stickers as desired.

9. Using industrial-strength glue, position and glue buttons to bottom corners of box.

Diamond Pattern
Full Size

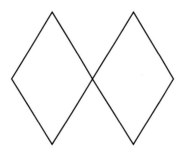

9
Cat Luster

Materials

Beads: small, variety (30)
Cards: die cut (3)
Embellishments
Glue: craft
Paper punch: small
Wire: 26-gauge
Wire cutters

How To

✳Refer to General Inst. on pgs. 6-18.

1. Using craft glue, glue cards closed.

2. Using paper punch, punch hole in top center of each card.

3. Embellish each card as desired.

4. Thread beads onto wire, twisting and bending wire as beads are added.

5. Thread beaded wire through punched out hole in top of each card. Twist wire together to secure.

In Other Words

Cards of any shape or size can be used to make small ornaments or gift tags.

July

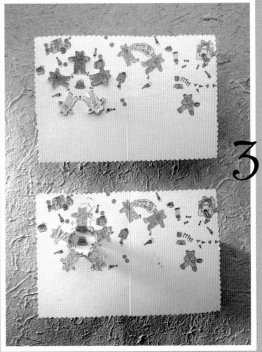

2

3

1

1
Seashell Journal

Materials

Acrylic spray sealer
Card
Cardboard: heavy
 5½" x 8¼" (2)
Crystal lacquer
Embellishments
Glue: découpage; hot
 glue gun and glue
 sticks
Paint: acrylic
Paintbrushes
Paper: handmade,
 5" x 8"; plain white,
 5⅜" x 8⅛" (40)
Paper punch
Raffia: ⅔ yd.
Texture medium

How To

✳Refer to General Inst.
 on pgs. 6-18.

1. Tear handmade
paper to fit top of one
cardboard piece for front
book cover.

2. Using découpage
glue, découpage
handmade paper to
cardboard.

3. Tear card to fit in
center of handmade
paper. Découpage card to
handmade paper.

4. Mix acrylic paint
with texture medium.
Apply mixture to card in
desired areas for
appearance of sand and
water.

5. Using hot glue
gun and glue stick, hot-
glue embellishments to
card.

6. Apply crystal
lacquer to highlight
desired areas for
appearance of water
drops on waves and sea
shells.

7. Apply spray sealer
to front cover of journal.

8. Center and punch
two holes through
cardboard front and back
and plain white paper,
2¾" apart and ½" from
top edge.

9. Place desired
number of plain white
paper sheets between
front and back covers.
Thread raffia, back to
front, through punched
holes. Tie raffia into bow
on front cover of journal.

In Other Words

Make a journal to
hold favorite funny
sayings.

2
Clay Coasters

Materials

Acrylic gesso
Acrylic spray sealer
Cards: (2)
Crackle medium
Flowerpot saucers:
 4"-diameter,
 terra-cotta (2)
Glue: découpage
Paint: acrylic (6)
Paintbrushes
Scissors: paper edgers

How To

✳Refer to General Inst. on pgs. 6-18.

1. Apply acrylic gesso to saucers.

2. Using acrylic paint, basecoat saucers.

3. Apply crackle medium to saucers. Apply topcoat to saucers.

4. Apply spray sealer to saucers.

5. Using paper edgers, cut cards slightly larger than inside bottom of saucers.

6. Using découpage glue, découpage cards inside saucers. Apply three coats of découpage glue to top of cards, allowing glue to dry between applications.

In Other Words

Coasters are great to give for white elephant or gag gifts.

3 Place Mats

Materials

Card: with art that can be cut and folded up
Cloth: soft
Glue: craft
Knife: craft
Paintbrush: old
Paper punch: ⅛"
Wire: 28-gauge, 12"
Wire cutters

How To

✳Refer to General Inst. on pgs. 6-18.

1. Laminate card.

2. Using craft knife, cut around edges of characters that need to stand. *Note: Do not cut all way around characters. Leave bottom of characters uncut.* Bend characters forward.

3. Using paper punch, punch holes on each side of characters.

4. Using wire, thread one end of wire through two side holes. Twist wire to secure. Bring other end of wire up and twist to form a balloon. Continue all way around holes to form a nut cup.

5. When party is over, cut wire and lay characters flat. Wipe place mats clean using soft wet cloth. Dry, and store for next party.

In Other Words

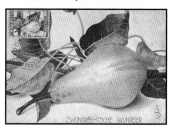

Place mats can be made as special mats for a plate of cookies or a favorite vase.

July

I WAS RICH, IF NOT IN MONEY, IN SUNNY HOURS AND SUMMER DAYS.   HENRY DAVID THOREAU

4

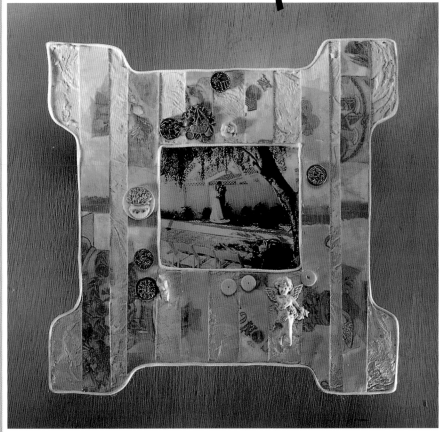

IT IS SUMMER, GLORIOUS DEEP-TONED SUMMER, THE VERY CROWN OF NATURE'S CHANGING YEAR WHEN ALL HER SURGING LIFE IS AT ITS FULL.
AMY LOWELL

4 Set of Frames

Materials

Acrylic gesso
Buttons: antique, various
    shapes and sizes
Cards: (4)
Cording: ⅛"-wide satin,
    1 yd. each frame
Glue: craft; hot glue gun
    and glue sticks
Jigsaw
Paint: acrylic
Paintbrushes
Paper towels
Sandpaper: fine-grit
Scissors: craft
Spackling compound:
    ready-mix, ½ pint
Wire cutters
Wood: ¼"-thick masonite

How To

✳Refer to General Inst.
  on pgs. 6-18.

1. Transfer Frame Patterns to wood. Using jigsaw, cut out patterns from wood. Sand cut out patterns.

2. Apply spackling compound to frames creating texture, following manufacturer's instructions. Let spackling compound dry thoroughly.

3. Using fine-grit sandpaper, sand frames.

4. Apply acrylic gesso to frames.

5. Using craft scissors, cut out strips or artwork from cards.

6. Using craft glue, glue strips or artwork to frames.

7. Using acrylic paint, wash frames including artwork areas. Wipe off excess paint with paper towels.

8. Glue satin cording around edges of frames.

9. Using hot glue gun and glue stick, hot-glue buttons to frame. If needed, cut back of buttons off with wire cutters.

Frame Patterns
Enlarge 240%

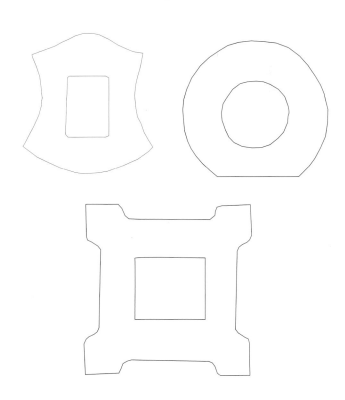

2

1

3

Stool
1

Materials

Acrylic gesso
Acrylic spray sealer
Antique medium
Cards: (3-4)
Glue: découpage
Paint: acrylic (7)
Paintbrushes
Paper towels
Scissors: paper edgers
Stool: wooden

How To

✳Refer to General Inst. on pgs. 6-18.

1. Apply acrylic gesso to entire stool.

2. Using acrylic paint, basecoat entire stool.

3. Using paper edgers, cut out artwork from cards.

4. Using découpage glue, découpage artwork onto top of stool as desired.

5. Using a fan brush, apply cross hatch strokes (stroke down, then across using darker colors toward outside and lighter colors toward inside) onto stool and slightly on artwork.

6. Apply antique medium to stool. Be certain to go around artwork well. Remove excess antique medium with paper towels. Apply spray sealer to stool.

In Other Words

Try découpaging anything from a foot stool to a high chair to decorate.

Fish Screen
2

Materials

Acrylic gesso
Cards: (2-3)
Embellishments
Glue: découpage; hot glue gun and glue sticks
Mat board: 16" x 44"
Paint: acrylic
Paintbrush
Paper: wrapping
Ruler
Scissors: craft
Screen: pre-made, folding
Sponge: old

How To

✳Refer to General Inst. on pgs. 6-18.

1. Apply acrylic gesso to screen.

2. Using acrylic paint, basecoat screen with one thin coat of paint.

3. Using craft scissors, cut out four pieces from mat board to fit behind screen openings. Using ruler, measure and cut wrapping paper to cover front of each mat board.

4. Using découpage glue, apply to back side of wrapping paper. Glue wrapping paper onto mat boards.

5. Using hot glue gun and glue stick, hot-glue covered mat board pieces to back of each screen opening.

6. Cut out artwork from cards. Cut sponge into tiny squares to place on back side of artwork for 3-dimensional appearance.

7. Hot-glue sponge squares to back side of artwork. Hot-glue artwork onto screen. Hot-glue embellishments onto front of screen as desired.

3 Tile Boards

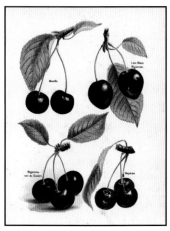

Materials

Acrylic gesso
Acrylic spray sealer
Cards: (3-4)
Clamps: (4)
Frame: wooden, unfinished, 9" square
Glue: découpage; wood
Knife: craft
Paint: acrylic (5-10)
Paintbrushes
Resin: high-gloss
Scissors: craft
Spray stain: walnut
Wood: ⅛"-thick pine, 4" x 4" (4) for tiles; ½"-thick pine, 9" x 9" for base

How To

✳Refer to General Inst. on pgs. 6-18.

1. Apply acrylic gesso to frame, base, and tiles.

2. Using wood glue, glue tiles to base, ½" in from edges of base leaving ⅛" between tiles.

3. Clamp tiles to base until glue dries.

4. Using acrylic paint, basecoat between tiles and along edges of tiles. Basecoat top of each tile with coordinating paint color. (Model was basecoated with antique white acrylic paint, then watercolored on top of each tile to coordinate with artwork.)

5. Apply light coat of walnut spray stain.

6. Using craft scissors, cut out artwork from cards.

7. Using découpage glue, découpage artwork to tiles, overlapping artwork as desired. Using a craft knife, trim excess artwork between tiles and around edges of tiles. *Note: Apply several coats of découpage glue to artwork to seal before applying resin.*

8. Apply resin to top of tiles following manufacturer's instructions. Smooth and thin resin between tiles with tip of paintbrush handle or stir stick.

9. Basecoat frame same color used between tiles and along edges of tiles. (Model has corners of frame watercolored to match top of tiles.)

10. Apply light coat of walnut spray stain to frame. Apply several light coats of spray sealer to frame.

11. Using wood glue, glue frame to base.

August

O Lord, who delivered me a fine June and a less fine July, help me get through August somehow.
R. Bradbury

A cow in the meadow
shakes her bell
And the notes cut sharp
through the Autumn air,
Each chattering brooke bears
a fleet of leaves
Their cargo the rainbow.
Amy Lowell

Summer afternoon, to me those have always been the most beautiful words in the English language.
by Henry James

79

4 Pine Cone

Materials

Bell cap: ¾" gold
    filigree
Cards or envelopes: (2-3)
Glue: craft; hot glue gun
    and glue sticks
Paint: acrylic;
    dimensional fabric
Paintbrush
Styrofoam egg: 3"
Thread: 4"

How To

✳Refer to General Inst.
    on pgs. 6-18.

1. Using acrylic paint, basecoat back of cards. Apply two coats.

2. Using Pine Cone Patterns, cut 25 large, 20 medium, and 20 small petals from cards.

3. Pattern on card should be to inside and paint to the outside. Roll four large petals from side to side over paintbrush handle. Gently straighten, leaving some curve.

4. Using craft glue, run a small bead of glue along four large pine cone edges from petal point to petal base. Press pine cone edges together to form four-sided shape that becomes pointed end of pine cone.

5. Using hot glue gun and glue stick, run a bead of hot glue around open end of pointed end of pine cone and press onto pointed end of Styrofoam egg.

6. Curl remaining petals around paintbrush handle, painted side up. Gently flatten except for petal tip.

7. Beginning row one underneath pointed end of pine cone with large petals, hot-glue petals in spiral pattern around egg, slightly overlapping at edges. Cover approximately two-thirds of Styrofoam egg.

8. For row two, hot-glue one large petal and one medium petal next to each other around egg. Repeat until row two is complete.

9. For row three, hot-glue medium petals around egg until row three is complete.

10. For row four, five, and six, hot-glue small petals until each row is complete.

11. Using acrylic paint, dry-brush over petals in random pattern.

12. Using dimensional fabric paint, dimensional paint petal tips. Let project dry for 12 hours before handling.

13. Place 4" length of thread through filigree in bell cap. Tie securely into loop. Hot-glue bell cap to broad base of pine cone.

Pine Cone Patterns
Enlarge 200%

Large Petal
Cut 25

Medium Petal
Cut 20

Small Petal
Cut 20

5
Bird Nest Box

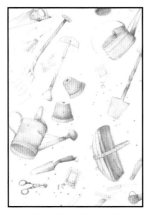

Materials

Box: wooden, 3⅜"
   square, 1½" deep
Card
Eggs: ¾" plastic,
   speckled (3)
Glue: craft, découpage
Knife: craft
Paint: acrylic
Paintbrushes
Paper: handmade, leafy
   design, ½ yd.
Scissors: craft
Spanish moss
Twig with leaves: small
Weeds: dried, variety

How To

✳Refer to General Inst.
  on pgs. 6-18.

1. Using craft knife, cut out artwork from card.

2. Using handmade paper and découpage glue, découpage paper to inside and outside of box lid and outside of box.

3. Using craft glue, glue artwork on outside and inside top of box lid.

4. Using acrylic paint, wash entire box. Wash box randomly using alternate color.

5. Découpage box and box lid, inside and outside.

6. Place Spanish moss and dried weeds inside box. Place eggs on top of moss. Glue twig to front of box.

In Other Words

Fill the bird nest with something unexpected like seashells or heart-shaped stones.

6
Tiny Book

Materials

Cards: (2-4)
Cord: 12"
Foam board: 2" x 3" (2)
Glue: craft
Paper: decorative, small
   pieces
Ribbon: ¾"-wide
   metallic
Scissors: craft
Sponge
Tape: brown paper, 12"
Trim: elastic cording, 6"

How To

✳Refer to General Inst.
  on pgs. 6-18.

1. Using craft scissors, cut one 3" strip of paper tape. Dampen tape with moist sponge.

2. Place two 2" x 3" pieces of foam board side by side. Join foam board pieces with damp paper

tape to make book. Fold book in half to make book spine and allow book to open and close.

3. Using decorative paper pieces, wrap and glue onto book covers and corners of book.

4. Cut artwork from cards. Add artwork, trim, and ribbon to outside front cover of book as desired.

5. Cut a card 5¾" x 2¾". Fold card in half. Center and glue card on inside fold of book.

6. Using 12" cord, make a loop and glue to back of book cover for hanger.

In Other Words

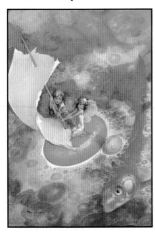

Small books are ideal for jotting down childhood memories, stories, and thoughts.

7 Howling at the Moon

Materials

Cards: (3)
Charm: ¾" brass
Foam board: 1½" x 2½"
Glue: craft; adhesive & sealant
Paint: dimensional fabric
Pin back
Scissors: craft
Wire: beading

How To

✳Refer to General Inst. on pgs. 6-18.

1. Using craft scissors, cut out artwork from cards. Cut two cards 1½" x 2½".

2. Using craft glue, glue two 1½" x 2½" cards to front and back of foam board for pin.

3. Using dimensional fabric paint, dimensional paint outside edges of foam board.

4. Glue artwork to front of pin.

5. Dimensional paint moon beam shape.

6. Using adhesive & sealant, attach brass charm in center of moon beam shape.

7. Using beading wire, wrap around pin area, top to bottom, side to side several times. Twist wire ends together to secure.

8. Glue pin back onto back of pin.

In Other Words

This easy to make pin can be made for everyday wear, holidays, or just a very special occasion.

September

When you wish upon a star
Makes no difference who you are
Anything your heart desires will come to you.

When your heart is in your dreams no request is too extreme
When you wish upon a star as dreamers do.

Fate is kind, she brings to those who love the sweet fulfillment of their secret longing.

Like a bolt out of the blue fate steps in and sees you through.

When you wish upon a star your dream comes true.

Ned Washington

1
Sweet Dreams Chair

Materials

Acrylic spray sealer
Cards: (3)
Chair: child's wooden
  pouting, 3 ft. tall
Glue: craft; découpage
Knife: craft
Paint: acrylic (5)
Paintbrushes
Paper towels
Pencil
Primer: oil-based, quick-
  drying
Ruler
Sandpaper: fine-grit
Spouncer: 1"
Stars: 2" wooden,
  whimsical (3)
Toothbrush

How To

✴Refer to General Inst.
  on pgs. 6-18.

1. Using craft knife, cut out artwork from cards. Set aside.

2. Using sandpaper, sand chair lightly.

3. Using primer, apply one to two coats on chair. Let dry.

4. Using acrylic paint, basecoat legs, chair back, and stars. Basecoat seat of chair.

5. Using pencil and ruler, mark seat of chair into 1" x 1" squares. Determine and mark placement of card. Using alternate color, paint every other square, omitting area of card placement.

6. Determine and mark placement of artwork on chair back.

7. Using one-part acrylic paint to three-parts paint color used on chair back, paint additional details as follows on model: For cloud design, crumple a paper towel into a ball. Dip into 1:3 ratio paint. Dab excess paint onto another paper towel. Randomly pat paper towel onto chair back for cloud designs. Using same 1:3 ratio paint and a flat paintbrush, make wispy streaks for clouds by artwork. Using small round paintbrush, randomly paint tiny stars on chair back.

8. Using contrasting paint color and toothbrush, splatter chair back.

9. Using découpage glue, découpage cards to chair seat and chair back.

10. Using craft glue, glue wooden stars to chair.

11. Apply two to three coats of spray sealer.

In Other Words

Do not forget to make a table to go with the chair or découpage cards on a closet door or front of chest of drawers to make the bedroom's decorating scheme complete.

September

Leaves may fall like rain, but young minds and hearts still rise to learn.

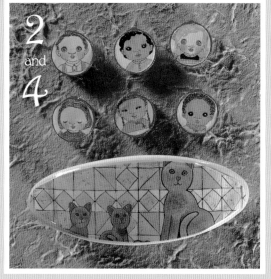

For off to school you must go,
To a little red house where they do know
How to read and write and teach wondrous things
Where friends you'll meet and songs you'll sing.   by Jo Packham

2
Button Covers

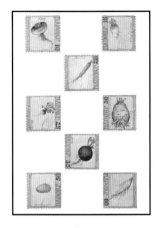

Materials

Button covers: ¾" metal (6)
Card: small pictures to fit on button covers
Glue: craft, découpage
Pencil
Ribbon: ¼" wide, satin ½ yd.
Scissors: craft

How To

✳Refer to General Inst. on pgs. 6-18.

1. Place button cover on card. Trace around button cover. Repeat for each button cover.

2. Using craft scissors, cut out pattern for each button cover.

3. Using craft glue, glue cut out pattern to each button cover.

4. Using découpage glue, découpage over each button cover.

5. Using craft glue, glue ribbon around edge of each button cover. Trim ribbon.

3
Bookend Chair

Materials

Acrylic gesso
Card
Doll chair: wooden, small
Fabric: denim, ½ yd.
Glue: découpage; hot glue gun and glue sticks
Paint: acrylic (3)
Paintbrushes
Scissors: craft; paper edgers

How To

✳Refer to General Inst. on pgs. 6-18.

1. Apply acrylic gesso to chair.

2. Using acrylic paint, basecoat chair. Paint edge of chair in checkerboard pattern using diluted acrylic paint.

3. Using craft scissors, cut back off of card.

4. Using paper edgers, cut out artwork from front of card to fit chair seat.

5. Using découpage glue, découpage artwork to chair seat.

6. Tear fabric into 1"-wide strips. Wrap around chair back and rails on bottom sides.

7. Using hot glue gun and glue stick, hot-glue ends of fabric to secure.

In Other Words

Make bookends match books such as kitchen cards for cook books.

4
Hair Barrette

Materials

Acrylic gesso
Card
Glue: découpage
Hair barrette: large with
    flat surface
Paint: acrylic
Paintbrushes
Pencil
Resin: high gloss
Scissors: craft

How To

✳Refer to General Inst.
  on pgs. 6-18.

1. Apply several
coats of acrylic gesso to
barrette.

2. Using acrylic
paint, basecoat barrette
with two coats of paint.

3. Place barrette on
card. Using pencil, trace
around barrette.

4. Using craft
scissors, cut out artwork
⅛" smaller than traced
line.

5. Using découpage
glue, découpage artwork
to barrette.

6. Apply resin to top
of barrette following
manufacturer's
instructions.

5
Chalk-
board

Materials

Acrylic spray sealer
Card
Chalk: white
Chalkboard: 7½" x 9½"
Glue: clear silicone
Hammer
Knife: craft
Nails: small (2)
Paint: acrylic
Paintbrushes
Sandpaper
Scissors: craft
Twine: thin, 19"

How To

✳Refer to General Inst.
  on pgs. 6-18.

1. Using acrylic paint,
basecoat chalkboard
frame.

2. Using sandpaper,
sand chalkboard frame
for worn appearance.

3. Using craft knife,
cut out artwork from
card.

4. Using hammer,
hammer two small nails
to top back of chalkboard
frame.

5. Using craft
scissors, cut one 9" and
one 10" piece of twine.
Tie each end of 9" twine
onto each nail for hanger.
Tie one end of 10" twine
to left nail to hang chalk
from. Tie chalk onto
other end of 10" twine.

6. Using acrylic
paint, write child-like
words and dot onto
chalkboard frame. Sand
words and dots for worn
appearance.

7. Cover chalkboard
and apply spray sealer
onto chalkboard frame.

8. Using clear
silicone glue, squeeze
three large beads on back
side of cut out artwork.
Lightly press artwork
onto chalkboard.

October

Listen! The world is rising,
And the air is wild with
leaves. We have had
our Summer evenings,
Now for October eves!

Humbert Wolfe

1
Hand-made Box

Materials

Card
Glue: craft
Pencil
Scissors: craft
Tracing paper

How To

✳Refer to General Inst. on pgs. 6-18.

1. Using transfer pattern and pencil, trace Handmade Box Pattern onto card.

2. Using craft scissors, cut out pattern from card. Bend card on dotted lines.

3. Using craft glue, glue edges of card together to secure.

In Other Words

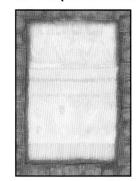

Boxes can hold travel memorabilia such as ticket stubs and match books.

2
Flower-pots

Materials

Acrylic spray sealer
Baking clay
Card
Flowerpots: 2½"-diameter terra-cotta (2)
Glue: craft; découpage
Paint: acrylic (8)
Paintbrushes
Scissors: craft

Handmade Box Pattern
Enlarge 200%

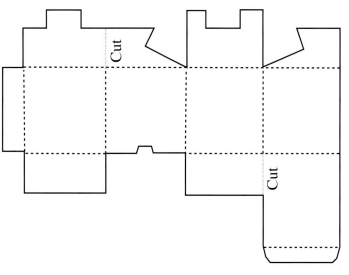

Cut

Cut

Flowerpots continued

How To

✳Refer to General Inst. on pgs. 6-18.

1. Using craft scissors, cut out 1"-wide strip from card to go around each flowerpot.

2. Using découpage glue, découpage strip around bottom of each flowerpot. Take small pleats toward bottom of flowerpot as pot tapers in. Apply several coats of glue over strips.

3. Using acrylic paint, basecoat rims and inside of flowerpots. Dot rims of flowerpots with coordinating color.

4. Using baking clay, roll into balls of various sizes. Form small balls in center of larger balls to form flowers. Roll clay into small strips and pinch ends and center to form leaves. Bake clay, following manufacturer's instructions.

5. Using acrylic paint, basecoat leaves and flowers desired colors.

6. Apply acrylic spray sealer to painted clay pieces.

7. Using craft glue, glue leaves and flowers around each flowerpot rim.

In Other Words

Cover a variety of flower pot sizes and shapes. For specific holidays, such as Christmas, cover flower pots with poinsettias and pine trees.

3 Stained Glass

Materials

Card
Chain: decorative for hanger
Copper foil tape
Flux
Glass: 6¼" x 4⅝" (2)
Glass cleaner
Glue: spray adhesive
Masking tape
Paint: acrylic; stained glass (5)
Paintbrush
Paper clips: (2)
Paper towels
Scissors: paper edgers
Soldering iron and solder
Suction cup hanger
Wire cutters

How To

❋Refer to General Inst. on pgs. 6-18.

1. Using paper edgers, trim around edges of card. Lay card on working surface, right side up. Center and place one piece of glass over card. Using masking tape, tape glass to working surface.

2. Using stained glass paint, apply onto glass using backside of card as guide. Make certain colors of paint touch each other and keep paint on card area within card edges. Let glass paint dry thoroughly. Remove masking tape from card. Using glass cleaner, clean both pieces of glass.

3. Using adhesive spray, apply to back side of card. Place back side of card onto painted glass. Place second piece of glass on top of front side of card. Be certain all glass edges are even.

4. Wrap copper foil tape around all glass edges. Apply flux over copper foil tape. Using soldering iron, solder around glass edges as desired, smooth or bumpy.

5. Using wire cutters, cut two paper clips ½" long to use as hooks for hanger. Solder paper clips to top back of glass edge.

6. Using a damp paper towel, wash entire project. *Note: Do not place under water. Glass may leak water inside card and paint.* Wipe glass dry.

7. Using acrylic paint, wash decorative chain. Loop chain through paper clips for hanger. Place suction cup hanger on window and place chain over suction cup hook.

In Other Words

Sometimes a thousand words are not enough!

These small pieces are so easy to make ornament size. Insert photos for a "family" tree or decorate for Christmas with bears and insert adorable bear cut-outs. They are perfect for a wedding invitation card.

4

4
Party Mask

Materials

Cards: (3-4)
Charms: (8-10)
Chain: decorative, 12"
Cord: metallic, 2 yds.
Eye mask: pre-made
Fabric: heart-shape,
    3" x 3½"
Feathers
Glue: craft; hot glue gun
    and clear and glitter
    glue sticks
Paint: acrylic
Paintbrush
Paper punch: ¼" hole
Ribbon: ½"-wide, 1 yd.
Scissors: craft

How To

✳Refer to General Inst.
    on pgs. 6-18.

1. Using craft scissors, cut one card width of eye mask with desired artwork on front.

2. Using paper punch, punch out shapes from another card. Punch hole in upper left and right corner of eye mask to attach ribbon to tie mask with.

3. *Note: Do not cover punch holes in mask.* Using craft glue, glue artwork onto eye mask, extending upward from eye mask. Glue shapes onto eye mask. Layer and overlap areas.

4. Using hot glue gun and glitter stick, outline eye areas and outside edges of mask and artwork.

5. Using hot glue gun and clear glue stick, hot-glue feathers onto top of eye mask.

6. Hot-glue charms, cord, and decorative chain onto mask as desired for embellishments.

7. Tie ribbon through punch holes in eye mask.

In Other Words

Masks can be made for ornaments, home accents, or to wear to a masquerade ball.

5
Cards On Canvas

Pictured on pg. 3

Materials

Acrylic gesso
Canvas: 11" square (3)
Color copy of cards: (3)
  (if writing on cards
  reverse copy)
Crackle medium
Paint: acrylic (4)
Photo transfer medium
Scissors: craft
Sponge
Staple gun and staples
Stretching bars: 9" (12)

How To

✳Refer to General Inst.
  on pgs. 6-18.

*Note: Stretcher bars
come in various sizes.
Canvas should be 2"
larger all around to fit on
stretcher bar frame.*

1. Using stretcher
bars, assemble frame
following manufacturer's
instructions.

2. Place canvas on
hard surface. Center
frame on canvas and
staple once on top and
bottom sides. Pull canvas
tight and repeat on
remaining sides.

3. Apply acrylic
gesso to canvas.

4. Using craft
scissors, trim color copy
of cards if necessary.
Apply photo transfer
medium to color copy of
cards. Place cards face
down centered on canvas.

5. Using acrylic paint
and sponge, basecoat
canvas around picture.

6. Apply crackle
medium to canvas around
picture and edges of
canvas.

7. Wash topcoat
around edges over
crackle medium. Allow
color to bleed slightly
onto edges of canvas.

In Other Words

Cards on canvas can have a
children's story theme or a western
theme.

October

6

7

6
Snap Out Of It

Materials

Acrylic gesso
Card
Drill with ⅛" bit
Glue: découpage; wood
Knife: craft
Paint: acrylic (4-6)
Paintbrushes
Pencil
Scroll saw
Sponge
Wire: 18-gauge bailing,
    ½ yd.
Wood: ½"-thick pine,
    14" square

How To

✳Refer to General Inst.
  on pgs. 6-18.

1. Using craft knife, cut out saying and artwork from card.

2. Using pencil, trace artwork onto wood.

3. Using scroll saw, cut out traced pattern. Cut out a 3" x 9¼" rectangle from remaining wood for sign.

4. Apply acrylic gesso to wood pattern and rectangle.

5. Using acrylic paint, basecoat wood pattern front and sides. Basecoat rectangle. Sponge rectangle with two contrasting colors. Paint desired design onto rectangle. Mark placement for saying on rectangle. Paint ¼" past mark to frame saying.

6. Using drill, drill a ⅛" hole in each top corner of rectangle. Thread wire through drilled holes. Bend wire in back to secure.

7. Using découpage glue, découpage artwork onto wood pattern. Découpage saying centered in painted frame. Apply a coat of glue over entire project to seal.

In Other Words

Any message can be conveyed with this easy-to-make, fun-to-give plaque.

7
Drawer Shelves

Materials

Balusters: 1¼" (8)
Cards: 1 per drawer
Drill with ¼" bit
Glue: découpage; wood
Knobs: (10)
Misc.: gold & silver
    leafing; acrylic paint;
    sponge
Molding strip: ¼" x ¾",
    66"
Nails: ¾" finishing
Paintbrush
Primer
Router: straight fluted,
    ¼" carbide with
    sharp bit
Sander: palm orbital
Sandpaper: fine-grit
Scissors: craft
Screws: dowel, ¼" (4);
    wood, #8 1½" flat-
    head (8)
Table saw
Tape measure
Varnish of choice
Wood: ½"-thick plywood
    for shelves, 13" x 33"
    (3); ¾"-thick #2 pine
    for drawer fronts and
    backs, 6" x 5⅞" (5);
¼"-thick birch
plywood for sides,
5⅞" x 12"; ¼"-thick
plywood for bottoms,
5⅞" x 12½" (20)

How To

❋ Refer to General Inst.
on pgs. 6-18.

1. Using table saw,
cut three 13" x 33"
shelves from ½"-thick
plywood. Cut balusters to
desired length. Measure
shelves and balusters and
adjust width of drawers
to the space available.
Allow space for easy
movement of drawers.

2. Cut five drawer
6" x 5⅞" front and back
pieces from ¾"-thick #2
pine.

3. Using a table
mounted ¼" carbide
router with a clean sharp
bit, cut rabbits on front
and back pieces ¼" x ½"
on three edges. This
makes it easier to fasten
sides and bottom.

4. Cut twenty 5⅞" x
12½" drawer side pieces
from ¼" birch plywood,
which yields a drawer
13" deep. Cut ten 6" x
12½" drawer bottom
pieces from ¼" plywood.

5. Using wood glue,
glue sides and bottom
pieces together. Using ¾"
nails, nail in place.

6. Using sander and
sandpaper, sand all
pieces.

7. Measure, mark,
and drill four drilling
holes for 1½" flathead
wood screws for top and
bottom baluster supports.

8. Measure, mark,
and drill four ¼" holes for
center shelf and use ¼"
dowel screws.

9. The back of
shelves require ten 6"
stop strips cut from
molding. Nail and glue to
back behind shelves to
prevent shelves from
sliding out the back.

10. Apply primer to
entire project. Using
acrylic paint, basecoat
project.

11. Using craft
scissors, cut out artwork
from cards to fit drawer
front. Using découpage
glue, découpage artwork
to front of drawers.
Wrapping paper can also
be découpaged to sides
of drawers.

12. Refer to painting
technique books for
supplies and methods for
antiquing, distressing,
faux finishes, gilding,
marbleizing, sponge
painting, and washing
techniques. Paint,
découpage, or gild each
drawer as desired.

13. Apply several
coats of varnish of choice
to project.

14. Add knobs to
drawers.

November

1

Thanksgiving in my house had nothing
to do with the pilgrims. Alberto Ríos

2

4

3

Come, ye thankful people, come.
Raise the song of Harvest-home.
All is safely gathered in,
Ere the winter's storms begin.

Henry Alford

Bird House
1

Materials

Acrylic spray sealer
Antique medium
Birdhouse: 5" x 5¼"
Card
Cloth: soft, clean
Glue: craft
Knife: craft; putty
Marker: watercolor
Paint: acrylic (5)
Paintbrushes
Pencil
Sandpaper: fine-grit
Spackling compound:
   ready-mix
Wood: ½"-thick balsa,
   ¹⁄₁₆" x 12"

How To

✳Refer to General Inst.
   on pgs. 6-18.

1. Using putty knife, apply thin layer of spackling compound to all surfaces of birdhouse except bottom.

2. Using sandpaper, lightly sand spackled sections of birdhouse.

3. Using craft knife, cut balsa wood into twelve ½" x 4" (or to fit length of roof) strips for roof.

4. Using craft glue, glue balsa strips to roof of birdhouse horizontally.

5. Using pencil mark 2½" from bottom around birdhouse.

6. Using acrylic paint, basecoat bottom of birdhouse. Basecoat upper portion of birdhouse one color, painting circle around birdhouse opening. Basecoat bottom portion of birdhouse another color. Basecoat roof and eaves, and perch another color. Dot around birdhouse opening for flowers. Paint "HOME" above perch.

7. Using watercolor marker, add lines around dots for leaves.

8. Using antique medium and cloth, apply to birdhouse following manufacturer's instructions. Wipe off excess.

9. Cut out artwork from card. Glue artwork onto back of birdhouse.

10. Outline around edges of artwork with paint.

11. Apply spray sealer to entire birdhouse.

In Other Words

The back of a card can be used. Simply cut off the bottom.

2
Mosaic Bowl

Materials

Acrylic spray sealer
Bowl: wooden, 6"
    diameter
Candle: pillar
Cards: (4-6)
Charms: ½" metal stars
    (20)
Paint: acrylic
Papier mâché: instant
Scissors: craft
Wax paper

How To

✳Refer to General Inst.
  on pgs. 6-18.

1. Using craft scissors, cut cards into ½"-¾" irregular shapes.

2. Mix papier mâché, following manufacturer's instructions. Mix acrylic paint into papier mâché for desired color.

3. Using fingertips, apply papier mâché to inside of bowl. Push pieces of cards and charms into papier mâché.

4. Place piece of wax paper on working surface. Turn bowl upside down onto wax paper. Repeat Step 3 to outside of bowl.

5. Allow bowl to dry for 1-2 days.

6. Apply spray sealer to entire bowl.

7. Place pillar candle inside bowl.

In Other Words

Bowls can be made in any shape and size with any combination of colors. Try a pastel bowl, one with rust tones, or one that is all black and white.

3
Mosaic Vase

Materials

Acrylic gesso
Cards: (4-6)
Cotton swabs
Glue: reverse découpage
Knife: craft
Paint: acrylic (3)
Paintbrushes
Paper plate
Ruler
Vase: glass, clear, with
    opening large enough
    to insert hand

How To

✳Refer to General Inst.
  on pgs. 6-18.

1. Using two compatible colors of acrylic paint, place small amount of each paint on a paper plate. Dip paintbrush into each color of paint and apply

to bottom on inside lip of vase. Repeat this process on upper portion of vase. Let dry.

2. Using craft knife and ruler, cut fronts of cards into ½" squares.

3. Using reverse découpage glue, découpage squares to inside of vase making horizontal rows.

4. Using wet cotton swabs, clean excess glue between card rows.

5. Using acrylic gesso and acrylic paint, mix together to form a paste. Basecoat inside of vase. *Note: Do not use water in vase.*

In Other Words

Make vases bright, pastel, or black and white with a touch of color.

4
Surprise Bag

Materials

Card
Color copy of card:
    (if writing on card reverse copy)
Fabric: muslin, 7½" x 8½" (2)
Needle: hand-sewing or sewing machine
Photo transfer medium
Polyester fiberfill
Scissors: craft
Sponge
Thread: coordinating
Twine: jute, ½ yd.

How To

✸Refer to General Inst. on pgs. 6-18.

1. Apply photo transfer medium to color copy of card. Place card face down on one piece of muslin.

2. Using muslin pieces, place right sides together and stitch three sides using needle and thread or sewing machine.

3. Using fiberfill, stuff pillow to desired fullness.

4. Using needle and thread or sewing machine, stitch opening closed.

5. Using craft scissors, cut twine into four 4½" lengths. Tie each corner of pillow with a knot. Tie remaining length into bow.

In Other Words

Make a bag and fill with chocolate kisses.

5

6

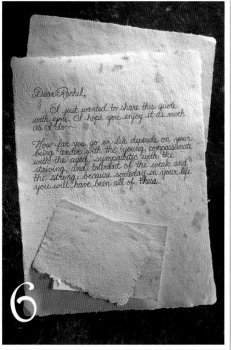

Dear Rachel,

I just wanted to share this quote with you. I hope you enjoy it as much as I do—

How far you go in life depends on your being tender with the young, compassionate with the aged, sympathetic with the striving, and tolerant of the weak and the strong; because someday in your life you will have been all of these.

7

5
Pear Bag

Why not go out on a limb? That's where the fruit is.

Materials

Box: size of bag
Card
Glue: découpage; hot glue gun and glue sticks
Knife: craft
Needle: large-eyed
Paper: handmade, 20" x 20"; hand-made, 5"x 8"; hand-made, 3"x 3"
Paper hole punch
Scissors: craft
Yarn: needlepoint cotton, (1 skein)

How To

✳Refer to General Inst. on pgs. 6-18.

1. Using hot glue gun and glue stick, fold and hot-glue 20" x 20" handmade paper around box, like wrapping a present. Leave one end of paper open. Slide box out of open end. Fold bottom of paper to form rectangle. Crease sides on bag to look like a paper bag.

2. Using craft knife, cut out artwork from card.

3. Using découpage glue, découpage artwork onto 5" x 8" handmade paper. Tear paper as desired around artwork.

4. Découpage 5" x 8" paper with artwork onto front of paper bag.

5. Refer to Herringbone Stitch Diagram on pg. 18. Using hole punch, yarn, and large-eyed needle, herringbone-stitch bag closed.

6. Using 3" x 3" handmade paper, fold paper in half to form triangle. Unfold and fold in half to form a rectangle. Unfold and fold in half in other direction to form another rectangle. Unfold and push up in middle so triangle goes into the center and make a crease.

7. Using hole punch, punch hole in top of triangle.

8. Open note card and write message on 3" x 3" handmade paper. Tie note card onto yarn and attach to front of bag.

6
Recycled Paper

Materials

Blender
Blotter papers: or newspapers covered with paper towels
Card backs: (6)
Dish pan: large
Envelopes: (6)
Iron
Paper stabilizer powder
Paper towels: (1 roll)
Staple gun and staples
Stretcher bars: 8" x 10" (2 pkgs.)
Wax paper
Window screen: 10" x 12"

How To

✳Refer to General Inst. on pgs. 6-18.

1. Using stretcher bars, assemble frame following manufacturer's instructions.

2. Place window screen on hard surface. Center frame on screen and staple across top side. Pull screen tight and repeat on remaining sides.

3. Tear envelopes and card backs into small pieces. Discard pieces with writing on them. Soak in warm water several hours.

4. Fill blender ½ full with water. Add ¼ to ⅓ cup soaked paper pieces. Blend on medium speed then on high until finely blended into pulp. Pour pulp into dish pan. Continue until 1 gallon of pulp has been mixed.

5. Add water to dish pan and pulp to within 3" of top of dish pan. Add paper stabilizer powder following manufacturer's instructions. Stir with hand.

6. Using a scooping motion, submerge frame in water, wood side up. Lift frame from water, catching pulp on screen. Let water drain for a few minutes.

7. Set frame, screen side down, on blotter papers. Using paper towels, pat excess water from pulp.

8. Using wax paper, tear piece to fit screen. Place over damp pulp and carefully turn screen over so pulp and wax paper fall free.

9. Let pulp dry on wax paper. When pulp is still slightly damp, remove from wax paper and press pulp with warm iron.

Plate 7

Materials

Acrylic spray sealer
Card
Foam brush
Glue: découpage
Gold leaf adhesive
Knife: craft
Paint: acrylic (2-4)
Paintbrush
Plate: glass, clear
Silver leafing
Sponge
Varnish: clear

How To

✳Refer to General Inst. on pgs. 6-18.

1. Clean plate. Using craft knife, cut out artwork from card.

2. Using découpage glue, découpage artwork to back inside bottom circle of plate.

3. Using foam brush, apply gold leaf adhesive to back of plate. Allow to set one hour.

4. Using silver leafing, break apart and apply onto gold leaf adhesive.

5. Apply acrylic spray sealer onto back of plate.

6. Using acrylic paint and sponge, sponge desired colors onto back of plate as desired. Basecoat back of plate using several coats of acrylic paint for full coverage.

7. Using varnish, seal back of plate. Apply several coats.

In Other Words

3

4

2

1
12-Point Star

Materials

Cards: (6-9)
Glue: craft
Knife: craft
Needle: hand-sewing
Pencil
Scissors: craft
Star: papier mâché,
    12-points
Thread: coordinating

How To

✳Refer to General Inst.
on pgs. 6-18.

1. Using pencil, trace one star point onto card.

2. Using craft knife, cut out sixty triangles from cards.

3. Using finger tips, apply thin layer of craft glue to triangle and glue to star. Repeat with each triangle in a random pattern until star is covered.

4. Using craft scissors, trim any excess card from star when completely dry.

5. Using thread and needle, push threaded needle through one star point. Secure thread and hang 12-point star as ornament.

2
Wreath

Materials

Cards: (3-5)
Charms
Embellishments
Fabric: 1 yd.
Glue: craft; hot glue gun
    and glue sticks
Ribbon: ½"-wide
    metallic, 4-5 yds.;
    ⅛"-wide satin, 4-5
    yds.; ¼"-wide metallic
    gathered, 4-5 yds.
Scissors: craft

Tassel
Wreath: 12"-wide,
    Styrofoam ring

How To

✳Refer to General Inst.
on pgs. 6-18.

1. Tear fabric into 2"-wide strips.

2. Using craft glue, apply glue to backside of one 2" strip. Tightly wrap strip around Styrofoam ring. Glue strip ends securely. Repeat until ring is completely covered with fabric.

3. Wrap ribbons around ring as desired. Glue ribbon ends securely.

4. Using craft scissors, cut out artwork from cards. Using hot glue gun and glue stick, place and hot-glue artwork cut outs, charms, and embellishments onto ring.

5. Make hanging loop from 4" piece of ribbon. Hot-glue to top backside of ring.

6. Hot-glue tassel and ribbons at bottom front of wreath as desired.

3
Card Keeper

Materials

Card: large
Crystal lacquer
Embossing pen
Embossing powder:
    metallic gold
Paper hole punch
Ribbon: 1"-wide plaid,
    2 yds.
Scissors: craft

How To

✳Refer to General Inst.
    on pgs. 6-18.

1. Using paper hole
punch, punch holes along
edge of card 1" apart.

2. Using ribbon,
leaving a tail of 15" for
bow, whip-stitch along
sides and bottom through
front and back of card.

3. Whip-stitch along
top, through front then
through back of card.
End on opposite side
leaving a tail of 15" for
bow.

4. Tie tails together
for bow.

5. Apply crystal
lacquer to card as
desired.

6. Apply metallic
gold embossing as
desired.

4
Music Folder

Materials

Card
Fabric: ¾ yd.
Glue: adhesive & sealant;
    hot glue gun and glue
    sticks; spray adhesive
Knife: craft
Mat board: 12" x 9"
Paper: corrugated,
    10" x 15"
Ribbon: 1½"-wide wire-
    edged, 1 yd.

How To

✳Refer to General Inst.
    on pgs. 6-18.

1. Using craft knife,
cut out artwork from
card. Cut mat board into
two 7³⁄₁₆" x 5" pieces.

2. Place fabric face
down on working
surface. Place mat board
pieces in center of fabric
with ⅛" between pieces
to allow for fold line.

3. Apply spray
adhesive to back side of
both mat boards. Fold
and wrap edges of fabric
to back side of mat
board.

4. Using hot glue
gun and glue stick, run a
bead of hot glue down
raw edges of fabric. Bend
loose fabric between mat
boards for fold line.

5. Fold corrugated
paper in half. Wrap and
hot-glue ribbon 1" from
inside left page around to
front of page, leaving
6½" ribbon on bottom
front of card. Hot-glue
covered mat boards onto
bottom inside of
corrugated pages. Wrap
and hot-glue 6½" ribbon
from front of corrugated
page around bottom of
covered mat board, lining
up ribbon. Hot-glue
ribbon on inside of mat
board to secure.

6. Hot-glue artwork
onto front of card,
overlapping ribbon
slightly.

5

6

7

5
Tree Ornaments

Materials

Cards: (2)
Copper foil tape
Flux
Glass: oval (2); rectangle (2)
Glue: craft
Paintbrush: old
Rag: old
Scissors: craft
Soldering iron and solder
Window cleaner

How To

✳Refer to General Inst. on pgs. 6-18.

1. Using window cleaner, clean glass.

2. Using craft scissors, cut out artwork from cards.

3. Using craft glue, place dots of glue around back of artwork. Position artwork on one piece of oval glass and one piece of rectangle glass. Center and place matching piece of glass on top of artwork.

4. Wrap copper foil tape around all glass edges. Apply two additional rows of copper foil tape around all glass edges.

5. Using old paintbrush, apply flux over copper foil tape. Using old rag, wipe excess flux off glass.

6. Using soldering iron, solder around glass edges until desired look is achieved. Build up areas to each side on top of glass to make rings for ribbon to hang ornaments.

7. Thread ribbon through rings. Tie in bow. Hang from tree or garland.

In Other Words

6
Card Holder

Materials

Acrylic gesso
Cards: (2)
Clamps
Embellishments
Fabric: velvet, 1½ yds.
Glue: adhesive & sealant; découpage; hot glue gun and glue sticks
Knife: craft
Paint: acrylic (3)
Pencil
Router
Scroll saw
Sponge
Wood: plywood: ¾"-thick, 6" x 3" for base; ½"-thick, 1¾" x 5¼" for support; ¼"-thick, 12" x 12" for front and back artwork

How To

✳Refer to General Inst. on pgs. 6-18.

1. Using craft knife, cut out artwork from cards for front and back of card holder.

2. Using pencil, trace artwork onto ¼" plywood for front and back of card holder.

3. Using scroll saw, cut out front and back patterns.

4. Using router, miter all sides of 6" x 3" wood base at 70° angle.

5. Apply gesso to front and back wood patterns.

6. Using acrylic paint, sponge all wood pieces with coordinating acrylic colors.

7. Using découpage glue, découpage artwork to front and back wood patterns.

8. Embellish front and back artwork as desired *Note: Sugar crystals were used on model for snow.*

9. Using hot glue gun and glue stick, hot-glue fabric onto plywood base and support.

10. Using adhesive & sealant, center, glue, then clamp front and back pieces onto fabric-covered support. Glue support to base.

7 Wooden Plaques

Materials

Cards: (2)
Glue: découpage
Hammer
Paint: acrylic (5)
Paintbrushes
Scissors: craft
Screwdrivers: large, flathead; Phillips head
Wood plaques: 5½" x 6" (2)

How To

✳Refer to General Inst. on pgs. 6-18.

1. Using hammer and screwdrivers, distress wood plaques, including edges.

2. Using acrylic paint and water, mix 2:1 ratio to make a stain. Using stain mixture, basecoat fronts of plaques vertically. Stain unevenly to create grain effect.

3. Using craft scissors, cut out artwork from cards.

4. Determine placement of cards 1¼"-2½" from bottom of plaques.

5. Basecoat bottoms of plaques. Basecoat sides and backs of plaques. Wash over front of plaques.

6. Using découpage glue, découpage artwork to front of plaques.

7. Paint desired words on front bottom of plaques.

In Other Words

December

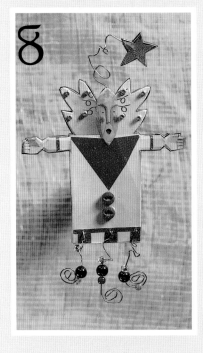

Somehow when Winter arrives, inspiration fills the air as tangibly as a child's breath on a frosty eve.

Nancy Lindemeyer

Some things have to be believed to be seen.

Ralph Hodgson

111

8
PMS Pin

Materials

Awl
Beads: 1mm gold (8); 1½mm transparent (3); 2mm black (3); 1½mm variety of colors (3)
Buttons: ¼" (2)
Card
Glue: adhesive & sealant; craft; découpage
Knife: craft
Magnet sheet: to fit artwork
Pin back
Scissors: craft
Wire cutters
Wire: thin, 26"

How To

✴Refer to General Inst. on pgs. 6-18.

1. Using craft knife, cut out artwork from card.

2. Using craft glue, glue artwork to magnet, leaving spot unglued at top of artwork to place wire.

3. Using craft scissors, cut out magnet around artwork.

4. Using wire cutters, cut one 2¼" length and three 2" lengths of wire.

5. Using adhesive & sealant, glue each end of 2¼" length of wire into top of artwork.

6. Using one 2" length of wire, curl one end of wire, leaving ½" on one end to place through awl hole in artwork. Thread one 1½mm variety of color bead, one 2mm black bead, and one 1½mm transparent bead onto wire. Repeat for total of three 2" lengths of wire threaded with beads.

7. Using awl, make three holes through bottom of artwork to place three 2" lengths of wire threaded with beads. Place wires through holes and bend down in back of artwork.

8. Using craft glue, glue two buttons and eight 1mm beads on front of artwork.

9. Using adhesive & sealant glue, glue pin back onto back side of magnet.

9
Gift Envelope

Materials

Card
Embossing powder
Envelope: blank
Fabric: 5" x 12"
Glue: hot glue gun and glue sticks
Heat gun
Needle: large-eyed
Pigment ink
Raffia: natural
Rubber stamps: (3)
Ruler
Scissors: craft; pinking shears

How To

✴Refer to General Inst. on pgs. 6-18.

1. Using craft scissors, cut back from card. Set aside.

2. Using pinking shears, trim front of card

edges and back flap of envelope. Measure front of card. Cut fabric to fit plus ¼" border allowance.

3. Using hot glue gun and glue stick, center and hot-glue fabric to front of envelope.

4. Using large-eyed needle and raffia, stitch card ¼" in from all edges.

5. Center and hot-glue card onto fabric.

6. Using craft scissors and back of card, cut out five squares to accommodate rubber stamp size.

7. Rubber stamp squares with pigment ink. Sprinkle with embossing powder, following manufacturer's instructions. Set embossing powder using heat gun.

8. Using pinking shears, cut five squares of fabric to accommodate stamped squares.

9. Hot-glue two stamped squares to fabric squares. Hot-glue two fabric squares to front of card. Hot-glue three fabric squares to back of envelope.

10. Tie three small bows from raffia. Hot-glue bows to bottom of each fabric square on back of envelope.

Note: This Gift Envelope was made for giving gift certificates, photos, or money. It is not suitable for mailing. If used for mailing, place into another envelope

10 Holy Cow

Materials

Angel wings: pre-made, paper, 5" x 2"
Card
Embellishments
Glue: craft; découpage; hot glue gun and glue sticks
Knife: craft
Milk bottles: miniature (3)
Paint: acrylic
Paintbrush
Pencil
Scissors: craft
Wire: ¹⁄₁₆" craft, 1 ft.
Wire cutters
Wood: ⅛" balsa, 8" x 6"

How To

✳Refer to General Inst. on pgs. 6-18.

1. Using craft scissors, cut out artwork from card.

2. Using craft glue, position and glue wings onto back of artwork.

3. Using pencil, trace artwork onto balsa wood.

4. Using craft knife, cut out artwork pattern from balsa wood.

5. Using acrylic paint, basecoat front and back of balsa wood pattern.

6. Glue artwork onto balsa wood pattern.

7. Découpage front and back of balsa wood to seal project.

8. Using craft wire, randomly twist wire to measure 7". Using wire cutters cut wire.

9. Using hot glue gun and glue stick, hot-glue one end of wire to back of artwork. Stick other end of wire into miniature milk bottle.

10. Embellish milk bottles as desired.

December

114

11 Ribbon Angel

Materials

Card
Glue: hot glue gun and
    glue sticks
Ribbon: 1½"-wide ombre,
    4½" (3)
Ruler
Scissors: craft
Thread: metallic gold, 6"
Tinsel: Christmas, mini
    ⅓ yd.

How To

✳Refer to General Inst.
    on pgs. 6-18.

1. Using craft
scissors, cut out artwork
from card.

2. Using hot glue
gun and glue stick, gather
ribbons by hand and hot-
glue to back of artwork.

3. Measure, cut, and
hot-glue tinsel to bottom
of ribbons and around
head of artwork.

4. Loop and hot-glue
metallic thread to back of
artwork head as hanger.

In Other Words

12 Angel Star

Materials

Beads: ⅜" (5); ¼" (5); ³⁄₁₆"
    (5); ½"; ½" long,
    thin (1 pkg.)
Bowl
Cards: (1-2)
Glue: craft; hot glue gun
    and glue sticks
Paint: acrylic
Paintbrush
Paper plate
Papier mâché: instant
Scissors: craft
Star: Styrofoam, 6" x ½"
Tinsel: Christmas, mini
    ½ yd.
Water

How To

✳Refer to General Inst.
    on pgs. 6-18.

1. Using craft
scissors, cut out artwork
from cards.

2. Using instant papier mâché, water, and bowl, mix papier mâché, following manufacturer's instructions.

3. Apply papier mâché to star.

4. Using acrylic paint, basecoat star while papier mâché is still wet.

5. Using craft glue, run a bead around edges of artwork. Press cut out artwork into center of star.

6. Glue two rows of ½" long thin beads around center artwork and along edges of star points. Glue ⅜", ¼", and ³⁄₁₆" beads at tips of each star point.

7. Using tinsel, twist once and fit as hanger for star. Hot-glue ends of tinsel to star points to secure. Hot-glue ½" bead to top star point of hanger.

In Other Words

13
8-Point Star

Pictured on pg. 119

Materials

Beads: ½" (8); 1½"
Cards: (1-2)
Glue: craft; hot glue gun and glue sticks
Paintbrush
Pencil
Ruler
Scissors: craft
Wire: 28-gauge jewelry
Wire cutters

How To

✳Refer to General Inst. on pgs. 6-18.

1. Using 8-Point Star Triangle Pattern and pencil, trace eight triangles onto front of cards.

2. Using craft scissors, cut out triangles from cards.

3. Using paintbrush handle, wrap triangle around paintbrush handle to form a tube.

4. Using craft glue, glue end of triangle to secure. Slide off paintbrush handle. Repeat for a total of eight tubes.

5. Using 5½" piece of jewelry wire, thread through ½" bead, two tubes, then another ½" bead. Twist ends together and push ends back into tube. Repeat three times.

6. Twist tubes and beads together to form a star.

7. Hot-glue 1½" bead to center of star.

8. Thread desired length of jewelry wire through one ½" bead for hanger.

8-Point Star
Triangle Pattern
Enlarge 125%

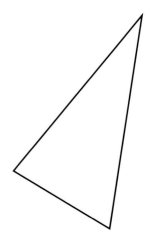

14 Santa Card

Materials

Batting: cotton, 1¼ yds.
Cards: (1-2)
Cording: ⅛"-wide satin
Craft stick
Embellishments
Glue: hot glue gun and
  glue sticks
Instant coffee in spray
  bottle
Marking pen: fabric
Ruler
Scissors: craft
Toilet paper tube

How To

✹Refer to General Inst.
  on pgs. 6-18.

1. Using craft scissors, cut batting into one 8" x 13" piece for body, two 5" x 8" pieces for arms, one 3½" x 5½" piece for hat, and two 2" x 3" pieces for cuffs. Cut out artwork from cards.

2. Mix 1 teaspoon of instant coffee with 2 cups hot water. Allow to cool. Place in spray bottle. Avoiding saturation, spray batting pieces front and back to give batting antique appearance.

3. To assemble body, measure up 1" from bottom right corner and mark with a dot using fabric pen. From bottom right corner measure over 3" and mark with a dot. Draw slightly curved line between two dots. Repeat for left side.

4. To assemble arms, roll one 5" x 8" piece of batting lengthwise into cylinder. Using hot glue gun and glue stick, hot-glue along raw edge to underlying layer to secure. Fold one 2" x 3" piece of batting in half lengthwise. Wrap cuff around end of arm. Hot-glue ends of each cuff together. Repeat for other arm and cuff.

5. To assemble hat fold batting in half widthwise. Hot-glue across one end. Turn right side out so seam is at back of hat. Fold front edge back ½" twice. Hot-glue together.

6. Hot-glue face onto craft stick. Hot-glue hat to face. Fold top of body down 1" twice for collar. Wrap and hot-glue body around toilet paper tube. Hot-glue craft stick inside of toilet paper tube. Push remaining batting at bottom of body into toilet paper tube. Center and hot-glue arm pieces to body back just below collar. Bring arms around to front and hot-glue edge of cuffs together.

7. Hot-glue artwork to Santa as desired. Embellish as desired. Tie cording around waist. Knot and fray ends.

In Other Words

15
Candle Wrap

Materials

Candle: 2¾" x 6"
Cards: (6-8); small
    pattern or solid color
Glue: hot glue gun and
    glue sticks
Paint: acrylic
Paintbrush
Ruler
Scissors: craft
Straight pins: (2)

How To

✳Refer to General Inst.
on pgs. 6-18.

1. Using ruler and craft scissors, measure and cut 3"-wide strip from small print or solid color card to fit around candle. Cut out desired artwork from cards.

2. Using hot-glue gun and glue stick, hot-glue artwork to 3"-wide strip, attaching larger artwork pieces first and filling in spaces with smaller artwork. *Note: Do not hot glue entire artwork to strip. Allow portions of artwork to stand free.*

3. Trim bottom edges of artwork to match straight edge of strip. Trim strip away from artwork as desired.

4. Using straight pins, pin one end of strip to candle. Gently wrap strip around candle and pin to secure.

5. Using acrylic paint, dry-brush exposed edges of artwork.

In Other Words

Candle wraps can make any candle a special gift. Make certain the card will not touch the area by the flame.

December

Christmas hath a beauty lovelier than
the world can show.
Christina Rosetti

119

16
Basket Card

Materials

Cards: (2)
Glue: craft
Knife: craft
Lace: ¼ yd.
Paper cup
Ribbon: ½"-wide, 1 yd.
Scissors: craft

How To

✳Refer to General Inst. on pgs. 6-18.

1. Using craft scissors, cut front of cards into eight ½" x 8" strips. Cut one ½" x 11" strip for handle.

2. Using craft glue, glue two strips on top of each other creating an "X". Continue gluing five more strips on top of first two creating a spoked effect.

3. Place strips in palm of hand and cup to form basket.

4. Glue remaining 8" strip around outside of spokes to hold basket shape. Basket may be set into paper cup to keep bands in place until glue is dry. Trim strips if necessary.

5. Glue 11" strip to sides of basket for handle. Wrap and glue ribbon around handle. Wrap and glue lace and ribbon around top edge of basket.

6. Embellish inside of basket as desired.

In Other Words

Make baskets for Easter, birthdays, or weddings.

17
Patch Work Coat

Materials

Baking clay
Broom: miniature, 8"
Cards: lightweight paper (5)
Card stock: 11" x 14"
Charm
Cotton ball
Double jump ring for earring
Fabric: 1" square (2)
Face mold
Glue: craft; decoupage; hot glue gun and glue sticks
Hair: curly, wool
Needle: hand-sewing
Paint: acrylic
Paintbrush
Papier mâché: instant
Scissors: craft
Thread
Trim: decorative, braid ¾ yd.

How To

✳Refer to General Inst. on pgs. 6-18.

1. Using craft scissors, cut large cone from card stock. Using craft glue, overlap seams ¼" and glue cone together.

2. Using baking clay and face mold, push clay into mold. Trim and smooth clay if needed. Remove clay from mold. Bake clay, following manufacturer's instructions.

3. Using acrylic paint, paint facial features on baked clay.

4. Mix papier mâché, following manufacturer's instructions. Pat over cone shape and smooth. Roll two thin strips of papier mâché, about diameter of a penny, 4" long for the arms. Form arms to cone body, bending at elbows and building up at shoulders.

5. Using craft glue, glue face onto cone body. Apply thin roll of clay around face to blend face to body.

6. Using craft scissors, cut cards into triangle and rectangle shapes. Using craft glue, glue card shapes to entire cone body. Apply coat of découpage glue to entire cone body.

7. Wrap small piece of cotton ball with fabric for mittens. Using thread, tie mittens securely. Trim excess fabric. Using hot glue gun and glue stick, hot-glue mittens at sleeve openings. Hot-glue hair on head of cone body. Hot-glue double jump ring to one side of hair for earring. Hot-glue decorative trim around collar area, sleeves, and hemline. Hot-glue charm to collar.

8. Using craft glue, glue broom between mittens.

9. Cut circle from card and glue to bottom of cone body.

In Other Words

Any styrofoam shape can be covered with papier mâché and découpaged with colorful card shapes to match your home decor.

18
Advent
Calendar

Materials

Card: 8" x 10" with
    paper dolls
Cutting board
Foam board: 8" x 10" or
    to fit card
Glue: craft
Jingle bells: ¼" (6)
Knife: craft
Marker: fine-tip,
    permanent
Ribbons: 1½"-wide,
    2 yds.; ⅜"-wide,
    1 yd.; ⅜"-wide, ⅓ yd.;
    ⅛"-wide, ⅓ yd.
Scissors: craft

How To

✳Refer to General Inst. on pgs. 6-18.

1. Using craft knife, cut foam board to fit card. Set aside.

2. Using craft knife and cutting board, cut through outline areas (leaving one section attached to open and close window) of card to make 25 advent windows.

3. Using craft glue, glue foam board to back of advent card.

4. Using marker, write activity under each window.

5. Using 1½"-wide ribbon, beginning at top of card and leaving 20" tails at each top corner, run ribbon around card edges.

6. String three bells onto two pieces of ⅛"-wide ribbon. Tie into a bow and glue to center of each top side of card.

7. Use remaining ribbons to embellish card as desired.

In Other Words

19 Place Cards

Materials

Cards: (desired number of place cards)
Gift tags: paper, 3" x 2"
Glue: craft
Knife: craft
Marker: metallic
Scissors: craft

How To

✳Refer to General Inst. on pgs. 6-18

1. Using craft scissors, cut out artwork from cards.

2. Using Place Cards Pattern, cut out desired number of place cards from gift tags.

3. Using craft glue, glue artwork to front top center pattern.

4. Using marker, outline around edges of artwork and front edges of gift tag. Write name at bottom of gift tag.

Place Cards Pattern Enlarge 165%

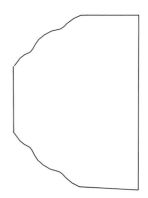

In Other Words

Card selection can vary for anniversary, birthday, or desired occasion.

December

20

21

23

22

On Winter nights beside
the nursery fire we
read the fairy tale,
while glowing coals build
pictures there before
our eyes. Amy Lowell

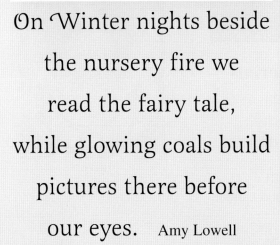

20 Folded Book

Materials

Card: horizontal scene
Embossing ink pen
Embossing powder
Heat gun
Needle: large-eyed
Paper: lightweight (2)
Ruler
Scissors: craft; paper
   edgers
Thread: gold

How To

✳Refer to General Inst.
  on pgs. 6-18.

1. Fold card in half widthwise, right sides together. Mark and fold card ½" from each side of fold so right side of card is out and forms a "W."

2. Fold both sheets of lightweight paper in half, widthwise. Using paper edgers, trim edges of paper to fit inside of folded card. Slip papers into each valley of outer card.

3. Using needle, pierce holes along spine of card and paper. Using needle with gold thread, bind the spine and papers together.

4. Using embossing pen, add details to front of book as desired. Sprinkle embossing powder over ink. Shake off excess powder. Use heat gun to set and raise embossing powder.

21 Candle Card

Materials

Cards: tri-fold; artwork
Embellishments
Glue: craft; rubber
  cement
Scissors: craft
Votive cup and candle:
  small

How To

✳Refer to General Inst.
  on pgs. 6-18.

1. Using craft scissors, cut out artwork from one card.

2. Using craft glue, glue artwork onto front of tri-fold card.

3. Open tri-fold card into triangle. Using rubber cement, glue triangle together. *Note: Rubber cement will allow card to come apart for storage.*

4. Embellish front of card as desired.

5. Set votive cup and candle inside card. *Note: Be certain candle is down far enough into votive cup to prevent flame from catching card on fire.*

In Other Words

22
Santa Box

Materials

Acrylic gesso
Baking clay
Box: papier mâché, 3½"
   square
Cards: (3)
Crystal lacquer
Glue: découpage
Paint: acrylic (5)
Paintbrush
Snow texture medium

How To

✳Refer to General Inst.
on pgs. 6-18.

1. Using cards and découpage glue, découpage entire box with cards.

2. Using baking clay, sculpt clay into form of boots, boot cuffs, hat, and hat cuff. Bake clay,

following manufacturer's instructions.

3. Apply gesso to clay pieces.

4. Using acrylic paint, basecoat boots and hat. Wash boots and hat.

5. Apply snow texture to boot cuffs and hat cuff.

6. Apply crystal lacquer to desired box parts for 3-dimensional effect.

In Other Words

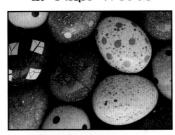

Make a box for every holiday. Easter can have rabbit ears and feet, Halloween a witches hat and boots.

23
Puzzle Box

Materials

Acrylic gesso
Acrylic spray sealer
Cards: (6)
Glue: découpage
Graphite paper
Masking tape
Paint: acrylic (8)
Paintbrushes
Pencil
Plastic wrap
Ruler
Sandpaper
Scissors: craft
Stain: water-based
Tracing paper
Wood blocks: 1¼"
   square (25)
Wood tray: 7¾" square,
   with center 6½"
   square"

Puzzle Box continued

How To

✳Refer to General Inst. on pgs. 6-18.

1. Apply gesso to wood tray and wood blocks.

2. Using acrylic paint, basecoat each side of wooden blocks with coordinating color of each card.

3. Using tracing paper, ruler, and pencil, make a grid with twenty-five 1¼" squares, five rows of five blocks.

4. Place grid over each card, one at a time, until desired design fills the grid. Place graphite

paper between card and tracing paper, shiny side down on card. Tape and trace grid onto card.

5. Using craft scissors, cut out squares from card. Label each square numerically.

6. Using découpage glue, découpage card squares onto coordinating painted side of each block. *Note: Check card square before découpaging to be certain it will match properly for the puzzle.* When all card squares have been découpaged to each side of blocks, trim card edges if needed.

7. Apply one thin coat of découpage glue to

each side of the blocks. Allow glue to dry thoroughly.

8. Apply spray sealer to each side of blocks.

9. Basecoat wood tray. Wash wood tray.

10. Wrap plastic wrap over wood tray, still wet, wrinkle with hands then carefully lift off plastic wrap. Apply coat of stain over wood tray and repeat plastic wrap technique.

11. Apply spray sealer to wood tray.

12. Sand edges of wood tray for worn appearance.

In Other Words

126

Index

Metric Equivalency Chart

mm-millimetres   cm-centimetres

inches to millimetres and centimetres

inches	mm	cm	inches	cm	inches	cm
⅛	3	0.3	9	22.9	30	76.2
¼	6	0.6	10	25.4	31	78.7
½	13	1.3	12	30.5	33	83.8
⅝	16	1.6	13	33.0	34	86.4
¾	19	1.9	14	35.6	35	88.9
⅞	22	2.2	15	38.1	36	91.4
1	25	2.5	16	40.6	37	94.0
1¼	32	3.2	17	43.2	38	96.5
1½	38	3.8	18	45.7	39	99.1
1¾	44	4.4	19	48.3	40	101.6
2	51	5.1	20	50.8	41	104.1
2½	64	6.4	21	53.3	42	106.7
3	76	7.6	22	55.9	43	109.2
3½	89	8.9	23	58.4	44	111.8
4	102	10.2	24	61.0	45	114.3
4½	114	11.4	25	63.5	46	116.8
5	127	12.7	26	66.0	47	119.4
6	152	15.2	27	68.6	48	121.9
7	178	17.8	28	71.1	49	124.5
8	203	20.3	29	73.7	50	127.0

Index